To Dad

"In, around, under and over the material universe, there broods an ineffable perfect Thinker; a sublime Artist seeking to perfect a flawed masterpiece."
William Rauscher

"Atheism is rather on the lip than in the heart of Man"
Francis Bacon.

"The mind is its own place, and in itself can make a heaven of hell, a hell of heaven."
John Milton

"The materialist assumption that spiritual substances do not exist is as much as act of faith as the religious belief in the reality of angels."
Mortimer Adler

"All secrets lie before us in perfect openness. Only we graduate ourselves against them, from stone to seer. There are no mysteries as such, only uninitiated of all degrees."
Christian Morgenstern

"Parapsychology is the Cinderella of the sciences. The stepmother, Science, has never favored her. She got a late start and the big sisters like physics, chemistry and biology almost cold-shouldered her out of recognition. It remains to be seen if any fairy prince will rescue her."
Louisa Rhine

Also by John Ronner:

Do You Have a Guardian Angel? And Other Questions Answered About Angels.

Know Your Angels: The Angel Almanac

The Angels of Cokeville

And Other True Stories of Heavenly Intervention

Published by:

Mamre Press
P.O. Box 3137
Murfreesboro TN 37133-3137

Library of Congress Cataloging-in-Publication Data
Ronner, John, 1951-
The Angels of Cokeville: and other true stories of heavenly intervention
p. cm.
Includes bibliographical references and index.
ISBN 0-932945-43-0
1. Angels -- Case studies. 2. Spiritualism -- Case studies.
I. Title
BL477.R658   1995
291.2'15 -- dc20   95-6334

Cover image: Annunciation to Joachim by: Master of Luebeck.
Credit: SuperStock

Manufactured in the United States of America

Table of Contents:

9. The feeling... 115

Story: A mother's prayer protects her sons from a gang of armed attackers by apparently making windows "invulnerable."

Essay: Premonitions, hunches, feelings... the "still, small voice within..."

10. The mysterious stranger... 121

Story: Chris Deal is a man broken by cancer. But then he -- and his wife -- suddenly see an angel in a hospital chapel that transforms them both.

Essay: The angel in disguise.

11. The animal... 131

Story: A golden retriever, crushed to death when a car topples off a cliff, comes back from death to help his injured master.

Essay: Spiritual intervention by animals.

12. The fragrance... 137

Story: Neither Terry Booker nor her visitors can explain the overpowering smell of magnolia in the Booker home until a certain name from her childhood pops into her mind.

Essay: Fragrances signaling the presence of the heavenly side.

13. The chorus... 143

Story: A Florida woman hears an angelic chorus after a night in which her marriage hangs in the balance.
Essay: Angelic music.

14. The gentle touch... 149

Story: A grieving 10-year-old Paul Swope, neglected by his father, needs to know that his beloved mother has not deserted him, even though she has died.
Essay: The heavenly caress.

15. The seen and unseen helper... 155

Story: A child says she rides with an angel to the hospital...
Essay: The celestial helper, unseen to some, yet visible to others.

Angel Directory... 161

Bibliography... 166

Index... 179

A Note From the Author

When I talk to an audience, the same questions about heavenly intervention crop up over and over. They go like this:

"When I had my near-death experience, I saw this dazzling figure of light. It was definitely something superhuman, infinitely wise and loving. Was this an angel? My personal angel?"

"My 'guardian angel' is my late husband. You won't believe it, but he still makes repairs around the house in the exact way he made them when he was alive. But I thought a guardian angel was supposed to be a superior being, not just a human spirit?"

"I had this irresistible gut feeling to make that call. When I did, I found out that my friend was contemplating suicide. Did an angel put that idea into my mind or was it something else?"

"I'll never forget the look on his face just before he died. He was actually talking into thin air, as if his wife, who had died two years ago, was standing beside the bed, waiting to take him. I'll always see the look on his face and the way he gestured. Was his wife an 'angel of death?'"

The terms "angel" and "guardian angel" are so loosely used that the words are defined differently by different people. And this haziness about what an angel is shows up in the polls. For example, in December 1993, Time magazine asked a scientifically selected sampling what they thought angels are: 55 per cent said, "Higher spiritual beings created by God with special powers to act as his agents on earth." (The strict definition.) But fifteen per cent felt they were the spirits of people who have died.

Seeing a dazzling figure of light, hearing invisible voices of warning or comfort, feeling overpowering hunches about things, having incredible coincidences happen, even being visited by departed loved ones -- all of these, and a lot more, have been attributed to heavenly intervention.

Here is a chapter-by-chapter, systematic look at the different ways people feel their lives have been touched by loving spiritual powers. Each chapter starts with a true story -- a powerful example of a particular genre of "heavenly encounter." Following that is an essay to put that type of experience in perspective for those who have had it and would like information about it.

But remember: Encounters with the angelic or divine are not just for saints and mystics or the simply fortunate. Every mundane moment is an epiphany, where light from heaven breaks through for those who have "eyes to see." Each of us is an experiencer at some level. Pay attention to your own epiphanies -- perhaps some of them within this book. But most of all, let your heavenly encounters, however subtle or dramatic, remind you that you are never really far from that "place of quiet rest, near to the heart of God."

-- John Ronner

Acknowledgments

Many people in this book have opened their hearts to me and shared their window on heaven. I have tried to lose as little of the power of their words and feelings "in the translation" to print as possible. My deep thanks to all of them. And a special thank you to Joan Nyberg, who helped me contact Tami Kriens, whose story also appears in different form in Joan's *A Rustling of Wings*, an "angelic guide" to Minnesota.

The Loved Ones...

For five years, the psycho genius David Gary Young nursed his plan to steal the children of Cokeville, Wyoming.

He plotted to take hostage every elementary child in town. He called it The Biggie.

And just like the medieval Pied Piper, a strange man who was angry at the town of Hamelin for spurning him, Young had no intention of ever giving Cokeville its kids back.

Instead, he would use his bomb to blast himself and all the youngsters through death's door -- to a Never Never Land in the afterlife. He called it the Brave New World or, in his diaries, BNW, for short.

On May 16, 1986, Young used a massive bomb to seize Cokeville Elementary School in the tiny Wyoming ranching hamlet of 550. This was the same town where Young had once been laughed at as a comic-opera town marshal.

Now, like a terrible relapse, he was back, far worse than ever. As investigator Ron Hartley would later put it, David Gary Young's thought processes and the rest of the world's were like two parallel lines that never met or intersected.

In Young's mind, the ignorant commoners around him never listened sufficiently to the all-knowing drifter who once wrote "philosopher" on a menial job application. But Young would now see to it that the entire globe paid rapt attention.

For starters, he demanded more than $300 million ransom for the 150-plus hostages crammed into a single classroom (a quarter of Cokeville's entire population) -- and a phone conversation with President Reagan.

Teachers tried not to show their fear in front of the children, but the students started crying and clinging, anyway, when Young began saying things like: "....Children are precious. I'll only shoot them with the .22" if he were disobeyed.

But uppity teachers would get a bullet from a rifle, he warned. It was academic, though. Secretly, Young was determined... once the ransom was in.... to blow up the children -- and himself, anyway.

As the scruffy Young saw it, the mass death would actually show his concern for the whimpering, praying youngsters in front of him. He and the pupils would be reincarnated in a higher dimension, the Brave New World. There, Young would rule these kids as the god of a new race. Their lying teachers who had deceived them would be replaced by a better mentor -- Young.

With his IQ. of 180 -- a towering but warped intellect -- this meticulous arrogant ex-cop had it all figured out. Right down to the bomb he carried in a shopping cart -- with the hair trigger. If anyone jumped him, a jerk of his wrist would take out much of the school while the armada of lawmen massed outside and the buzzing helicopters overhead looked on helplessly.

Within the small classroom under Young's loveless, steady gaze was nearly every child from kindergartner through sixth grader that Cokeville had.

Everything was figured -- except for the Angels of Cokeville. Heavenly beings that appeared at a critical moment to some of the hostage children.

Shortly before the bomb erupted into a searing orange fireball around 3:30 p.m., the atmosphere in the room for some seemed to change. Several children in different parts of the room -- independently of one another -- saw glowing beings appear or heard a telepathic voice speaking.

The long road to the Biggie started in the bomber's own childhood. Hardly a picture shows the young loner without a weapon in his hand.

Later, in a philosophy class at Chadron State University, the collegian Young began to developing his weird mystical ideas, including the Brave New World -- reachable only through death's door -- and the idea that he could prove mathematically that God does not exist.

This compulsive record keeper -- whose excruciatingly detailed diaries recorded his gas mileage, the food he consumed, how often he had sex (the Olympic pack rat even kept a used condom labeled "Margaret 1964") -- once scrawled on a card: "Evil makes the game. Love is nothing!" And in large letters, "ME! GOD! I do not exist. God does not exist. (How utterly simple)."

King Arthur had his sword Excaliber and David Gary Young had DGY-1, a .45-caliber revolver customized for him and containing his initials as its serial number. Of the hundreds of guns he owned, this favorite weapon became his bosom buddy, with whom he conversed in his diaries. They understood each other. Like Young, DGY-1 was hard, cold, and potentially violent, and one day, it would help enforce its master's philosophy... And, in the end, DGY-1 would propel him bloodily into the Brave New World.

By the 1960s, Young was already thinking about the Big Move, nicknamed The Biggie, that would force an unappreciative world at last to acknowledge his superiority:

At first, he toyed with, then rejected, the idea of hijacking a 747 jumbo passenger jet "with a few good people," as he put it.

In 1977, nine years before The Biggie -- Young came to Cokeville for the first time -- but as Barney Fife rather than Attila the Hun. As the freshly hired town marshal, this Keystone Kop wore a big western hat and had a long-barrel pearl-handled pistol tied down at the leg. The amused townfolk labeled him "Wyatt Earp."

One person who did believe in the headstrong Young was a submissive and insecure Doris Waters -- "Dorsie" -- an aging beauty who dreamed of a big career as a country-western singer but was limited to mundane gigs, such as at Cokeville's Red Dog Cafe and Saloon.

When the exasperated town fathers finally booted Young after only four months (Among other things, Young had the careless habit of twirling loaded guns in the presence of youth), the philosopher and his new found disciple rode off together on Young's motorcycle.

The domineering Young turned out to be a hard taskmaster for Doris. Once, for example, when Doris put on several pounds, Young reacted harshly. Stung by his words, Doris spent the night with another man. As her penance, Young required her to cruise the bars and procure for him two women.

It was in 1981, while a menial worker at a Soda Springs, Idaho mine, that Young began hatching The Biggie, his ticket out of a lifetime of frustration: Grab the above-average Cokeville kids; get the millions in ransom as a family-oriented Mormon town desperately tries to get those kids back; get even for the Wyatt Earp sneers; and finally, blow it all up. Then, like a pharaoh buried with his treasures and courtiers, Young would wake up in the afterlife with his millions, his dutiful wife, his beloved guns, his exhaustive diaries -- and the captive audience of kids. A resurrected Phoenix, listened to and respected at last.

In 1984, Young quit working altogether, leaving Doris to clean houses to support him while he spent full time "thinking."

Matters finally came to a head two years later. Young titled the first page of his 1986 journal: "Year of the Biggie." Doris wrote in her diary: "What will we do with the money? What will we be called in the new world?"

In March, the Youngs took a coast-to-coast, border-to-border farewell trip, a last pre-Biggie hurrah that Young's inevitable diary shorthand reduced to the "CC & BB."

On April 30, two weeks before the Biggie, the bomb maker's mini- Manhattan Project climaxed at Young's favorite desert getaway, aptly nicknamed "Blowhole." At Blowhole, Young successfully set off a homemade test bomb (built with the guidance of an off-the-shelf how-to-do-it bomb making manual). "And it comes down," Young wrote momentously.

On May 7, nine days before the Biggie, their marriage coming unglued, Doris wrote: "D (David) and I make love for the last time as husband and wife. Friends from now on. Changes."

With Doris at his side, Young mustered the other recruits for his task force: Bob Harrison, a former Nebraska police chief Young once worked for as a cop; former schoolmate Jerry Deppe; Young's 19-year-old daughter Princess; and Doyle Mendenhall, a former co-worker at the Idaho mine.

None of them had a clue what horror The Biggie actually involved. They were all misled by Young into thinking it was some vague money-making formula to "revolutionize the system."

On May 13, Young and his unwitting commandos converged at Cokeville's Red Dog Cafe, synchronizing watches at 5 p.m.

Young wrote his last diary entry on May 14: "And the plot thickens!"

Maybe it was the ex-cop in Harrison that caused him to get antsy at Young's coyness and split from the group. After that, Young finally briefed the rest of his troops about the real nature of The Biggie, his coming "revolution" to "beat the system" -- how he would collect ransom for the child hostages and then take the kids with him to "an island."

Doyle and Mendenhall flatly refused to have any part in the cruel madness. Young's teen-age girl started crying and said she just couldn't.

Young was never one to brook insubordination in the ranks. He handcuffed the two men to a back seat in the Toyota van, threatening to shoot both them and his unwilling daughter.

"It looks like it's just you and me, babe," Doris told her leader. Young put a gun in her hand.

When the rapidly shrinking strike force pulled up at Cokeville Elementary's side door around 1:30 p.m. May 16, Young forced Princess to help him and Doris deploy their arsenal and mini-library of personal diaries.

Minutes later, school secretary Tina Cook looked up to see a scraggly haired stranger with a long red beard, handguns jammed into his belt. He declared: "This is a revolution!... The lives of everyone in this school depend on you." The unkempt man showed her the bomb and its hair-trigger "deadman's switch."

Young had done his homework. The trigger was a clothespin. If jumped, all Young had to do was jerk his wrist. A shoestring tied to Young's arm would then pull out a piece of wood wedged in the mouth of the clothespin. The stick would be jerked out of the clothespin's "mouth." The jaws of the clothespin would snap shut. Two metal screws would come together, completing an electric circuit, and -- kaboom! -- the entire south wing of the school and everybody in it would be on their way to the BNW.

And so, an incipient knot of hostages began to form at the school office as ill-fated people, like a UPS delivery woman and a job applicant stumbled into the captive group or were corralled by a gun-waving Young as they passed by down the hallway.

As this first batch of hostages trooped down the hall to be herded into teacher Jean Mitchell's 30- by 30-foot first-grade classroom -- Princess, crying, suddenly shouted: "I can't believe you're doing this!"

Young threw her the keys to the van and snarled: "You're no longer my daughter. Get the hell out of here."

Screaming, Princess ran out of the school and drove off in Young's only getaway vehicle. What did Young care? *He would escape the school another way.*

An hysterical Princess rushed into the town hall. Her story tumbled out disjointed. Hurry, she blurted. Her father was crazy, but smart enough to make a bomb! She wished he were dead. *Get a cop!*

Gradually, they calmed her and pieced the horror story together. An initially skeptical Kevin Walker checked the van and, as Princess had said, there really were two greatly upset men inside, handcuffed to the back seat. *It was true!*

Doris prowled the school hallways, luring excited, study-weary classes to the hostage room with talk of a "safety demonstration" or a "big surprise."

The bright eyes dimmed when they entered Room 1 and saw odd things... a weird-looking, shabbily dressed stranger... the guns stacked along the chalkboard... the shopping cart that stank of gasoline. The kids were confused.

"I'm a revolutionary -- the most wanted man in this country," the red-bearded stranger bragged to the packed room. They were all his hostages, he said -- virtually everyone in the school. He wanted $2 million per hostage, a rap session with Reagen -- and any back talk from kids or grown-ups would be answered by a gun.

"Children are precious. We don't want to hurt them. I'll only shoot them with a .22 (pistol)," Young "reassured" the group. Teachers, on the other hand, would get the more deadly rifle. Their lives meant nothing, Young said. They had led these young minds astray. But now, he was here to give the kids a better role model...

As understanding dawned, some children started crying and sniffling. Others crouched in teachers' laps. "I don't want to be here," a little boy told teacher Kliss Sparks. Some kids vomited -- in waste paper baskets because Young was suspicious about trips to the bathroom.

Here and there, kids prayed together. Young didn't mind. Nobody was listening up there, anyhow.

Desks were pushed out of the hostage room to make more space.

"Do you realize what you're doing psychologically to these children?" Principal Max Excell asked Young. "They'll be scarred for life by an incident like this." Young was unfazed. They're bargaining chips, he explained.

The armed author passed out copies of a nonsensical manifesto of his philosophy -- copyrighted, no less -- quoting Shakespeare and Socrates and declaring that "zero equals infinity."

"Bullcrap," one captive reader concluded privately.

At the town hall "war room," it was a lawman's worst nightmare: an experienced ex-cop who was also a brilliant lunatic. The grand armada of police cruisers massing outside the school was no match for Young's little clothespin.

Radio stations got wind of the standoff from their police radios. The bad electronic vibes went out over the airwaves: 150 kids and 17 teachers and staffers trapped. A police cordon struggled to keep the press of milling parents at bay. Young said he'd shoot kids if anyone came near.

Then the media invaded: a satellite truck, eye-in-the-sky copters, almost as many reporters as townfolk. Phone lines were so tied up, many callers couldn't even get a dial tone. Outside, the cold grey Friday matched the soul of the man inside.

In the hostage room, Dorsie seemed more like a social director than a terrorist, scurrying here and there among the hostages, leading games, talking to kids. When the hostages tried to ease tension by singing happy birthday to first grader Jeremiah Moore, Dorsie laughed, then joined in.

"Think of this as an adventure you can tell your kids and grandkids about," Dorsie said incongruously, as if the cold-eyed shaggy stranger with the gun-crowded belt were Walt Disney and the hot crowded room some attraction at a summer theme park.

The kids got more and more restless. They crowded Young, got him nervous. He decreed a forbidden zone around himself, marked off with masking tape. The "magic square." Cross the "line of death," Young told the kids, and he would start shooting the grown-ups around them.

Time passed. Kids prayed, watched cartoons, cried, colored, trembled, drew pictures and vomited -- thanks to nauseating gasoline fumes from the bomb. Young allowed windows and doors to be opened for ventilation.

Young forced Excell to be his mouthpiece to the cops. No, he wouldn't dicker with negotiators. He was an ex-cop, he said, and he knew how they messed with your mind.

A couple of hours into the siege, Young started sweating profusely. Strangely, he seemed to be losing his air of assurance.

Young delicately transferred the hair-trigger to Dorsie's wrist while the anxious roomful of hostages held its breath. And then he stepped into the rest-room.

About that time, six-year-old Nathan Hartley was snapping together plastic toy pieces very close to the bomb. He happened to look up and saw something surprising: *Shining people, holding hands.*

The shining people floated downward through the ceiling, then hovered in the air, a mixture of young and old. *Why, they're angels!* Nathan suddenly realized. And everybody seemed to have one -- except for the mean stranger.

Nathan looked at the woman helping the stranger: Her angel was far away, way overhead, and seemed to be leaving, although all the other angels were so close to each hostage that they seemed almost perched on their shoulders.

The angels were nice -- smiling, shining like light bulbs. They made him feel good. Did he have an angel, too? He turned and almost yelled. A luminous woman was there with him. She said she was his great-grandmother. The bomb is about to go off, she told Nathan. Get up, go to the window, she warned. The strangers were about to die because what they were doing was wrong, she told him.

Nathan Hartley stood up and started walking.

At the same time, in another area of the room, Katie Walker, 7, and her sister Rachel, 9, were coloring near the TV. Suddenly, Katie noticed a glowing "family" dressed in white, descending into the room through the ceiling. The family floated in the air about two feet above the floor -- a man, a woman, another woman holding a tiny baby, and a small girl with long hair. They were "bright" but "brighter in the face."

The bomb is going off soon, the woman told Katie. She should do what her brother Travis was about to tell her to do -- stay by the window -- and she would be all right. Katie could feel the love coming from this strange lady.

Meanwhile, Travis, talking to friends on the opposite side of the room, heard a spiritual voice. *Get your sisters*, the voice told him. *Take them to the window, stay with them and everything will be all right*, the voice continued. Travis led the girls -- coloring books in hand -- to the window, not saying why.

Katie watched the glowing beings. They started moving away...

The kids in the room were noisy. Dorsie called for "quiet time." Then she turned suddenly to say something -- *too suddenly*. The string was jerked. *Two rapid booms*.

The lights went out. A huge orange fireball mushroomed inside the magic square. Tentacles of shooting fire rose up, arced and then showered the hostages. Choking, blinding black smoke filled the room.

A split-second of stunned silence from the hostages. Then: bedlam, chaos. Screaming hostages bolted for the doors, bumping and jostling. Some dropped to the floor. The fire alarm clanged over shouting voices: *"Get down!... Cover your mouth and nose! ... Get out! ... Run!*

Teacher's aide Verlene Bennion thought of her three grandchildren in the room -- and the other kids who were someone else's grandchildren, too. She would stay -- no matter what. Dropping to her knees she crawled through the smoke, groping for kids to shove out the windows.

A petrified Cindy Hartley, 9, was folded up on the floor in a fetal crouch. "Who's in here?" Verlene asked. *"Me!"* Cindy put out her hand. Verlene grabbed it.

Meanwhile, searing heat burned the arms of Pat Bennion as she joined Rocky Moore in feeling through the darkness for more kids. Like popping corn, the little ones rapidly tumbled through the windows -- pushed out by adults -- so fast the kids stacked up on top of each other below.

On the other side of the room, teacher Kliss Sparks smothered fire that was burning childrens' hair and clothes. Nearby, kids were clambering over furniture barricading one door. Janel Dayton started shoving the obstacles aside. Adults pushed kids out the door.

The heat began touching off loose ammo which Young had devilishly placed at the bottom of his bomb-laden shopping cart. Bullets snapped and whizzed through the room like fireworks, ricocheting.

Amid the pandemonium, Young came out of the rest-room -- DGY-1 in one hand and a .22-caliber pistol in the other. Suddenly, he and fleeing music teacher John Miller found themselves less than three feet apart. *Oh no! He's going to shoot,* Miller thought.

Miller turned and ran -- then felt the dull thud of a slug burying itself into his shoulder. The music teacher made it out of the school and collapsed near an ambulance. He survived.

Doris was a human torch. Pitifully, the doomed woman tottered toward her husband. Young aimed the bulldog .44-caliber pistol at her head and fired, splattering her brains onto the ceiling.

Now, Young backed up and crouched in the bathroom. Doris was gone. Screams all around from panicked children fleeing his trap. There'd be no revolution, no call from Reagan. Cops on the way.

Young turned to his last friend: DGY-1. He put it under his chin. It spoke its farewell forcefully.

Outside the school, the desperate crowd heard it: *Boom!* Then, an intervening split-second.

Then again -- *boom!* Black smoke belched out of the school's windows. A news reporter's running commentary broke off: *"The bomb has gone off!"* he cried to his audience. Spectators sobbed in each other's arms. The cordon gave away as hysterical parents rushed the school.

Then -- a sudden, eerie sound: *children screaming en masse.* Wild-eyed kids with soot-blackened faces -- except for white tear marks -- streamed out of the school's doors or spilled out the windows, little legs pumping frantically as they fanned out in every direction. Each small running body -- another gift from heaven to some parent, thought a frantic Claudia Hartley, who scanned the mob for her four children. "Oh, thank you, Lord -- that's one... That's two... three... four... Oh, Lord, how can I ever thank you?" she prayed.

Kindergartner Johnny King jumped on his bike: "I don't wanna die! I don't wanna die!" Whole families broke down sobbing as they embraced in knots. So many hugs and tears that one kid exclaimed: "I didn't know so many people loved me!"

A dozen ambulances screaming off to nearby hospitals was not enough. Paramedics loaded more shocked and burned hostages into schoolbuses escorted by wailing police cars.

"Sixth grade, meet by the tree... Has anyone seen Chad?"

As parents and teachers desperately tried to account for the hostages, a growing wonder began to take shape: Not a single hostage had died despite the bomb -- although the two kidnappers, who held all the cards -- were now permanently dealt out.

Sheriff's bomb expert Richard Haskell ran into investigator Ron Hartley. "What you've got here, Hartley, is a full-blown miracle," he said.

Young's reign of terror was over. The revolution had devoured its own.

After the bombing, townfolk became aware of one coincidence after another, some of them weird:

- Two weeks before Young pounced on the school, Cokeville Elementary had its first-ever fire drill practicing a mass evacuation -- on hands and feet -- from one room, the lunchroom.

- For months, a malfunctioning electrical panel kept shorting out, each time setting off the school's fire alarm -- causing an unplanned evacuation drill. But after the hostage-taking incident, the panel never malfunctioned again.

- The bomb had only exploded with a fraction of its force. Three of its blasting caps didn't ignite because wires to them were mysteriously cut. These three caps -- and a fourth one -- were supposed to push deadly aluminum powder into the air to cause a second, horrendous grain elevator-style dust explosion. But the fourth cap -- its wire intact and not cut -- also didn't ignite. It turns out the fourth cap was soaked with gasoline leaking from a jug. So the flammable powder never got into the air.

- Although ammo ricocheted wildly through the room, and the walls were peppered with pockmarks -- only one child was actually hit.

- The stench of gasoline leaking from the bomb caused the doors and windows of the hostage room to be opened, helping the bomb vent much of its explosive force.

- A group of civil defense workers just happened to be in town that day and just happened to be at the town hall when a hysterical Princess arrived. Cokeville mobilized quickly.

- The morning of the incident, a young girl inexplicably stubbornly refused to go to school, despite her mother's insistence.

Finally, the most unusual development of all: Some children told their families they had seen or heard spiritual beings in the hostage room just before the bomb went off. The kids were from two families that had not had contact with one another. Neither family knew about the other's mystical experience at first.

"They saved us. I said a prayer, and they saved us," Katie Walker explained. Looking through family photos, Katie suddenly became excited and pointed to a locket picture of her long dead great-grandmother, Shirley Ruth Thornock, identifying her as the kindly spiritual being who spoke to her.

After Katie spoke, brother Travis was encouraged to reveal his own experience -- hearing the voice that directed him to take his sisters away from the bomb.

In the other family, Nathan Hartley, too, kept his vision to himself at first, finally revealing it to a counselor working with hostage children to heal trauma. Sheriff's Deputy Ron Hartley, one of the investigators of the case and Nathan's father, was skeptical. He methodically questioned Nathan but could find no holes or inconsistencies in his unshakable story. Finally, Ron accepted it. In a manner similar to Katie's, Nathan identified a picture in a photo album as the spiritual being who spoke to him: Flossie Elliott, his great-grandmother who had died at age 93 when Nathan was 3.

Word circulated through town that still other children besides the Walker and Hartley kids had seen or heard otherworldly things in the room

"The evil that men do lives after them..." said Shakespeare. In their dreams, Young still stalked the children. Nathan Hartley woke up at night screaming: *"Let me go! Let me go!"*

On Sunday, two days after the Biggie, parents and their blistered and bandaged kids packed the church pews. In one sanctuary, the singing of the hymn Count Your Blessings... Count Them One by One... faltered as voice after voice choked. One girl put her bandaged arm around her weeping mother and patted her softly.

"To say it was a miracle would be the understatement of the century," said bomb expert Richard Haskell.

Essay: The Guardian Spirit

"Oh, blest communion, fellowship divine! We feebly strug-gle; they in glory shine. Yet all are one in Thee, for all are Thine. Allelujia! Allelujia!" **For All the Saints**

If death is truly a "dawn upon black waters" -- do dead loved ones not only live on but sometimes come back to us temporarily from "that heavenly shore?"

The church phrase "the communion of the saints" refers to the spiritual bond linking the living on earth and the dead in heaven as sung about in the above hymn For All the Saints -- a bond that cannot be severed even by the loss and grief of death.

And polling makes it crystal clear that tens of millions of us believe that they have experienced a tearing of the veil and a glimpse of the other side -- if only for a brief reunion.

In a 1973 scientific poll by the National Opinion Research Center at the University of Chicago, more than one fourth revealed that they believed they had been in touch with someone who died. And just over half of the widows and widowers questioned said they had.

Summing up the results of that poll, reported in a national Associated Press wire story, one headline writer trumpeted: Contact With the Dead 'Almost Common'. The famous Catholic priest and sociologist Andrew Greely commented matter-of-factly: "Over 50 million people have such ex- periences; six million have them often."

In most cases, this living-dead contact is fleeting, often just a single incident. The contact usually occurs be-tween loved ones -- parents and children, siblings, spouses -- and is particularly likely to happen around the moment of someone's death.

The living-dead encounter becomes a chance to say good-bye, to tie up loose ends ("I just wanted to say I'm sorry about what I did, but I love you and I'll see you again someday..."), or perhaps to deal with the two great fears of Western culture: the nightmare of hellfire or, at the other extreme, the nightmare of extinction of consciousness at death. ("Look, I'm alive -- death is not the end, and I'm not in pain!")

Sometimes, there's a need to take care of unfinished business. In 1925, for example, a court case was fought over the alleged appearance of a North Carolina farmer's spirit to one of his sons to help him find a missing will. After the court battle, farmer James Chaffin's will was declared valid.

When the departed show up, though, it's not always just for family or close loved ones, however. An Illinois woman, Susan K. Fine, told author Suzy Smith how, as a seven-year-old child, an invisible hand gripped her left arm hard as she was about to accidentally tumble down a staircase that years earlier had killed a teen-age boy in another family. The hand gripped her so hard as it pulled her backward that it left a swollen red mark visible on the arm, and Susan's crying summoned her father. Only later did her father, James Davis, admit that he had seen a smiling young boy behind Susan who vanished as she turned around to see who had caught her, finding nobody there. Susan's brother, Timothy "Jay" Davis, told Ms. Smith: "We talked about it a lot when I was growing up."

"It looks as if this little spirit boy may have remained in the house for some time, possibly because he enjoyed the company of the children in the family. At least, he was there when he was needed to perform his guardian angel stint," Smith comments in *Life Is Forever.*

As in the Cokeville story and the Fine account above, there is often circumstantial evidence that an actual visit occurred -- not a mental trick to help the bereaved soothe themselves. The evidence may be multiple witnesses. Or, two people separated by even thousands of miles, may share the same experience:

For example, it's common for a survivor to report seeing a dying loved one's spirit at one location a brief moment or so after the death has occurred at another place miles away. In other cases, two or more witnesses may see the specter, then compare notes favorably on their separate observations after the visit -- even witnesses in different locations!

A typical evidential case was reported by evangelist Billy Graham, referring to an article that originally appeared in Reader's Digest:

A well-known Philadelphia neurologist, S. W. Mitchell, was awakened by a young, upset girl knocking at his door, asking him to go with her into the bitter cold outside. Although exhausted, Mitchell dressed and followed her. Eventually, he entered a home and found a woman seriously ill with pneumonia. When Mitchell complimented the woman on her daughter's alertness and persistence, the woman was taken aback and told the doctor that her daughter had died a month ago. Mitchell went to a closet where the late daughter's coat was still hanging and found the very coat worn by the young girl who had awakened him just a short time earlier -- but the coat here was dry and warm. Although Graham wondered whether an angel had taken the form of the young daughter, others might argue that it was the daughter herself, reaching out from beyond the veil to help her mother.

Norman Vincent Peale, whose hugely popular book *The Power of Positive Thinking* has influenced an entire culture, revealed in 1977 how he had briefly been in contact with his late mother, father and brother on separate occasions. At a large Methodist meeting at Sea Island, Ga., at the request of moderator Bishop Arthur J. Moore, several hundred clergyman began marching forward, singing, to the front of the meeting room. Peale, sitting on the speaker's platform, looked down on the throng and saw his late father walking among them, according to Marton Ebon, a noted writer on parapsychology themes.

"I saw him as plainly as I ever saw him when he was alive. He seemed about 40, vital and handsome. He was singing with the others. When he smiled at me and put up his hand in an old familiar gesture, for several unforgettable seconds, it was as if my father and I were alone in that big auditorium. Then, he was gone, but in my heart, the certainty of his presence was indisputable," Ebon quoted Peale as saying.

Peale is not the only modern notable to peek beyond the veil. Actor Peter Sellers, who said he more than once has spoken with his dead mother, and Methodist Church founder John Wesley, who had lively conversations with the dead in his dreams, are two among many others.

In a minority of cases, people report that a lengthy after-death relationship between the departed and the survivor develops, a bond that sometimes continues indefinitely. A Florida widow once declared to me matter-of-factly that her late husband continued to do repairs around the house in the same manner in which he had done them while living!

The late parapsychology writer D. Scott Rogo reported a 1971 study by Welsh physician W. Dewi Rees who went into unusual detail as he interviewed 293 London widows and widowers. Reese learned that almost half of them believed that they repeatedly interacted with dead spouses. Fourteen percent said they saw apparitions, 13 per cent allegedly heard them speak, 12 per cent reported having conversations and three per cent claimed they had been touched, according to Rees, whose findings were published in the British Medical Journal.

Skeptics are often completely unaware how common is beyond-the- grave contact and guardianship because these happenings are kept close to the vest by experiencers who don't want their heartfelt or even sacred moments trivialized as neurochemical overloads, wishful thinking and so on.

Sometimes, one spouse has had contacts while the other spouse is a skeptic, unaware of the mate's experiences.

Belief in departed loved ones or ancestral spirits watching over the home was widespread in ancient times. Romans, for example, routinely offered food at mealtime to the Lares -- protective household spirits whose chief was the ghost of the family's founder. Archaeologists digging in the ruins of 5,000-year-old Sumer, the world's first civilization, have found altars in the homes for honoring household spirit guardians.

Still, despite the high frequency of alleged living-dead contact in modern times and the circumstantial evidence in some of these encounters, skeptics still routinely argue that visions of the departed are just hallucinations to comfort the bereaved.

Shakespeare personalizes this tension between the believer and the skeptic in his play *Hamlet*. There, Hamlet is thunderstruck to see the ghost of his murdered father. He tells his friend Horatio, who pooh-poohs the very idea. And so, Horatio becomes Shakespeare's symbol for the skeptic, Hamlet a symbol of the believer.

Later in the play, the two friends are together and -- of course -- here comes the ghost again, this time for both to see. Hamlet then turns to a shaken Horatio, perhaps with some self-satisfaction, and utters those famous words that have echoed through English literature as the classic rebuke to the materialist: "There are more things in heaven and earth, Horatio, than are dreamt of in your philosophy."

2. The Living Helper...

In Vietnam-era 1970, a young collegian, Jack Wheeler, met a beautiful Texas coed, Delores Miller, and both knew at first sight that they would marry. A blissful romance began. But right after the knot was tied, Jack won Lyndon Johnson's lottery. His number four brought a grim jackpot: a trip to hell.

It was hard for Jack and Delores to be apart, even in Texas. And now, just a few months later, he was 12,000 miles away from her in Nam, a jungle infantryman, surrounded by mud, soaking rain, mosquitoes -- and Charlie...

Yet, in a way Jack has never completely understood, Delores was with him through his battlefield horrors, a beckoning guardian angel, appearing at critical moments. From this, Jack knew inwardly he would never receive a Dear John letter from the beautiful woman he had left behind.

One of those critical moments was at Camp Eagle in March, 1971, when Delores apparently gave Jack a life-saving wake-up call.

Camp Eagle, a jungle base camp of the 101st Airborne, was just south of the DMZ. Jack was off duty, sleeping in his fatigues on a cot inside his "hooch" -- a crude hut -- while someone else guarded the camp perimeter. Still, Jack kept his rifle hugging his side -- a steel security blanket.

Lying next to Jack was Midnight, a black dog that had escaped being an entree on a Vietnamese dinner table and had been adopted by the GIs. (Stray dogs flocked to American troops because the Vietnamese ate them).

Around 2 a.m., Jack groggily started to wake up. In his still-hazy mind, Delores somehow seemed to be there talking to him. *Get up, Jack! Leave the cot!* she seemed to be saying. Jack opened his eyes. In front of him was a floating figure, hovering about a foot above the ground.

It was Delores! But taller. And her hair was blowing around.

Delores reached down and grabbed Jack's arm, tugging at him. Jack got up. Almost sleepwalking. He did not even bother to put on his boots. He walked out of the hooch 10 or 12 feet. Then, suddenly: a loud explosion behind him...

The concussion knocked Jack to the ground face first. He snapped out of the trance instantly. Two more explosions to the rear. Jack, now completely alert, looked around. There was Midnight alongside him. The dog was gripping his arm with its jaw. Midnight had been pulling him away from the hut!

But what about Jack's vision of Delores? In some strange way, did Midnight have help -- an ethereal assistance which Jack would never be able to explain? Jack looked behind him. His hooch and its cot had been obliterated. An enemy shell had landed right on top of his bed. Very close to it were the craters of two other shells.

In November 1970, a chopper pilot friend of Jack's had just picked up the mail from a clerk in the rear and brought the correspondence to his buddies in the jungle. Jack got Delores' letters, delivered all at once in a bundle of seven.

Jack stepped into the copter to join a small scouting party. The chopper then lifted to take the group deeper into the jungle. Meanwhile, Jack kept his seven letters close by -- an umbilical cord to a distant, sane world.

The plan was to drop Jack's reconnaissance unit in the hinter lands. There, they would infiltrate enemy-held areas, probing for Charlie's movements and positions, finally radioing back the info. But things never got that far.

The first strange event was the appearance of a brown, lazily meandering river, sliding below the rapidly moving chopper. Looking down from his seat, Jack noticed that the brownish waters were exactly the color of Delores' brunette hair. A small wooded island in the river formed itself into the image of her face. Delores' face beckoned to him.

As Jack leaned out of the copter, looking downward, he heard her voice: *"Don't worry, Jack. I'm here to protect you."* The palm trees below formed part of a green-and-white blouse.

At that moment, one of Delores' seven letters fell to the floor, landing right by his feet. Jack reached for it. But wind blew the letter to a new spot. He reached farther. The letter was blown to a spot still farther. The third time, Jack had to stand up and step away from his seat to try to fetch the letter. Now, the letter was blowing out of a chopper window.

Jack moved still farther away from his seat to try to grab it before it was lost for good. At that instant, a series of enemy rounds ripped through the seat where Jack had been sitting -- before Delores' flitting letter had led him away. Jack fell forward. The bullets grazed his legs.

Jack was unhurt, but the copter was crippled and began tumbling downward. Everything went black. Later, Jack came to. His copter had crashed into the top of a high tree in the middle of the wooded island -- the "mouth" of Delores' face. The chopper lay precariously on its side. *Careful.* Any sudden movement could shift the copter's massive weight, jar it loose from the treetop and send it plummeting 50 feet, or even further if it bounced off the cliff below.

Jack checked the interior and saw bodies. Most of the crewmen were dead. He noticed that he had taken shrapnel himself. Jack looked down. Delores was below, rising up from the ground, her arms outstretched, reaching toward Jack. *"I'm here to protect you,"* she said.

Suddenly, the chopper began shifting and slipping. It dropped. Jack jumped clear of it. His body slammed the ground five stories below. More unconsciousness.

Now, he was in a tunnel leading to the afterlife -- an inverted cone filled with incredibly spectacular colors. He was rushing toward its far end. The cone got smaller and smaller as it tapered. The colors more and more gorgeous as he advanced. A extremely bright whiteness mesmerized him. Jack felt chill bumps from the awesome thrill of moving through this tunnel -- a thrill that increased moment by moment. *Go faster!*

The ecstasy and euphoria were like winning the jackpot of a $50 billion lottery. Every worry, fear, problem... drained away as he moved along the inverted cone. His soul and his mind were being washed free. *Delores!*

Suddenly, she was there, a transparent half-figure -- from the waist up -- blocking his way. She was still colored brown as she had been at the river. Jack's headlong rush ground to a halt. But he looked beyond her -- down the tunnel. He saw the end of it: Magnificent sparkling stars. The pot of gold at the end of the rainbow! Jack wanted to move on, but Delores stretched out her hands to him. *"Don't leave me,"* she said. ' *'I want you to come home -- to have children with you. If you don't stop, you'll never see me again. You'll lose me!"* Delores said.

Delores was larger than life. Jack rested himself in her bosom. She held the battle-weary GI. like a child in her arms. Floating through the tunnel, Delores carried Jack backward through the tunnel, reversing his motion. The brilliant colors faded, became bland, washed-out. The two came back out of the front of the tunnel and moved into a dazzling light...

Sometime later, Jack opened his eyes. He was in a hospital room. *What had happened?* A rescue copter had come, they said, picked him up and brought him here. But all of the soldiers on the crashed chopper were dead -- except him. Jack checked a precious asset: the letters from Delores. They were all there -- *including the seventh letter that had blown out of the chopper.*

In 1971, Jack struck up a friendship with Fred, a member of his scouting patrol. Both GIs liked 1950s-style rock music. Fred, a photographer, dreamed of going to California after the war to work in films. Fred's girlfriend had just broken up with him. But he took genuine delight in Jack's good fortune -- at having someone special waiting on the home front. Delores, Fred said, might even become a movie star with her looks. This was just like Fred to say that. Fred was a cheery optimist, a relief to Jack from the negativity that so-often infected the careworn GIs around him. The two spoke excitedly of their futures -- away from Nam.

One day, important news came in. Someone had heard about abandoned underground tunnels dug by the North Vietnamese in the vicinity. Soon afterward, a helicopter lifted off, ferrying a six-man reconnaissance patrol led by Jack, and including Fred, into the jungle. Their mission: Find the exact location of the empty tunnels so they could be bulldozed.

The terrain was too rough for the chopper to land. Jack, Fred and the others hopped off the copter's skids to the ground, crouching, as the rotor's wind swirled the vegetation.

The foliage was thick as they moved along. As they approached the tunnels, shots rang out. *An ambush!* The tunnels were not empty, after all. Two patrol members crumpled, killed instantly. Jack, Fred and two other survivors fell behind logs and brush for cover. They radioed for the chopper to come back.

Then, a bullet tore open Fred's stomach, but he was still alive. Desperately, Jack took off his pants and stuffed them into the hole to stop the bleeding. As the enemy threatened to encircle the three survivors, Jack ordered the patrol remnant to fall back to a better protected area.

Jack stood up, draped Fred over his shoulder, turned his back and began carrying Fred out of their shelter. More gunfire. A round went into Fred's back, finishing him. But Fred's body had shielded Jack's back from a fatal wound, although shrapnel cut into Jack's leg and foot.

Jack, despite risking his life to save his friend, was racked with guilt.

Two days later, Jack was back at base. Another mission loomed. Amid a monsoon downpour, helicopters were lifting off with soldiers headed for the bush.

As Jack stepped aboard one copter, it was so overloaded, with two dozen soldiers, that it was too heavy to rise. Two servicemen needed to get off. *Not me*, Jack thought. *Might as well stay on the copter and get this over with.*

But a man in fatigues came to the door of the copter, called Jack by name, and told Jack and another soldier to step off. He and Jack did. Jack looked more closely at the man. *It was Fred!* Suddenly, Fred was gone. And the other soldier -- who stepped off the copter with Jack -- walked off to a mess hall, acting like he had never seen Fred.

Jack turned to cross a gully of gushing water, and Fred was there again, as suddenly as he had vanished. Standing in front of Jack in a clean uniform -- Fred was completely dry, despite the downpour all around. A solid, 3-D specter.

"Don't feel sorry about what happened," Fred said, his thoughts telegraphing themselves directly into Jack's mind without any speech. Fred referred, of course, to the round of gunfire that had killed him. "Don't feel guilty. It was heroic of you to try to save me."

"What are you doing here? Where'd you come from," Jack thought. Fred responded: "I just wanted to talk to you one last time." Fred lightened the situation by remarking that he still had the pants Jack used to stuff the wound. That struck Jack as funny, and he laughed.

"You can accomplish anything you want to, Jack," Fred said. "The most fun you can have in life is to dream dreams and then make those dreams come true."

Fred had dreamed of Hollywood film-making but now found himself among a different starry host, yet he still enjoyed the thought of his friend's ambitions, as he had on earth. Now, Fred looked ahead and previewed Jack's future.

"You're lucky to have Delores," he said, but there would be marital problems. Guard against inflexibility, learn to be more accommodating. Be understanding about these problems in the marriage, and it will continue successfully, Fred foretold.

"I'm leaving, Jack. You'll never see me again. But I've spoken to Delores. She's going to watch out for you and protect you."

Jack was soaked to the bone and cold in the heavy shower. Then, suddenly, the rain stopped. The sun came out. Simultaneously, Fred was gone.

Three hours later, Jack heard that Alpha Company was missing. These were the soldiers he was about to helicopter away with when Fred had called him off the chopper. Still later came terrible news: the chopper had crashed into a mountainside. All aboard were killed.

On Oct. 28, 1972, after these and other spiritual interventions, 23-year-old Jack Wheeler went home to his young wife, who was unaware of her exploits a half world away.

2. Essay: Phantasms of the Living

Ghosts of the departed are a familiar idea, of course. But less well-known is that persons sometimes claim to see the phantasm of a living person, called a *double*.

Doubles are said to be spiritual or mental copies of the living person. They may be translucently ghostly or three-dimensionally solid to the eye -- in the latter case often fooling witnesses.

Generally, doubles are spotted somewhere other than where the living person happens to be. These duplicates are often reported to be non responsive, acting abnormally or wooden as if not really aware -- other times acting rationally and with intent.

Traditional thinking holds that the double of a person, in some cases, is part of the living person's soul, seen psychically by others. In some instances, the theory goes, a double may appear because a person is traveling out-of-body in astral form, either intentionally during a self-induced trance or, more usually, unintentionally, particularly while sleeping.

But other explanations are also offered: The person seeing the double might just be picking up a telepathic image of someone who is thinking intently of the observer or who is thinking of being in the place where the observer finds himself physically.

In 1905, a bout with the flu kept British parliamentarian Frederick Carne Rasch from going to a debate he keenly wanted to attend. Nevertheless, two of Carne Rasch's parliamentary peers, Gilbert Parker and Arthur Hayter, said they independently spotted Rasch sitting in his normal seat during the debate. Hayter even mentioned his sighting at the time to a third M.P. As for Parker, he said he even spoke to the phantasm, not realiz- ing it was not real, and got no reply. When Parker looked back at the seat a moment later, Carne

Rasch was gone. Parker went out looking for him, unsuccessfully.

Later, when Carne Rasch finally did actually return to Parliament, he was irritated to find fellow legislators touching and poking him to make sure he was real. He said he was sure his "fetch" (as the Victorians called the double) had gone to the debate because he had very much wanted to be there.

Most projections of a person's double, like Carne Rasch's, are not intentional. And oftentimes, a crisis is said to bring about the projection. Parapsychology researcher Nandor Fodor cites a typical crisis story, published in *T.P.'s Weekly*:

A young British girl was taking the train to Cambridge to meet her fiancee. But she was startled to see, at every station where the train stopped, the ghostly double of her fiance, gesturing with a terrified look for her to get off the train. Finally, at one station, the apparition was gesturing even more wildly, and she decided to detrain immediately. Soon afterward, the train wrecked, and the car she was in was demolished. During all this time, her fiance was asleep in a waiting room at Cambridge and had no recollection of dreaming anything out of the ordinary.

The astral body of a sleeping person has commonly been believed to sometimes leave the physical body during sleep and wander. Fodor cites the following case, one of 701 examined in an 1886 book, *Phantasms of the Living*, produced by the respected Society for Psychical Research:

The Rev. P.H. Newnham reported a vivid dream. He saw the family of his fiancee, chatted with the father and mother in his dream, bade them good night, took a candle and went off to bed. On arriving in a hallway, he saw his fiancee near the top of a staircase. Newnham rushed up the stairs, passed his arms around her waist... Then, Rev. Newnham woke up, and a clock in his house struck ten almost immediately afterwards.

"So strong was the impression of the dream that I wrote a detailed account of it the next morning to my fiancee," Rev. Newnham wrote. "Crossing my letter, not in answer to it, I received a letter from the lady in question: 'Were you thinking about me very specially last night just about 10 o'clock? For, as I was going upstairs to bed I distinctly heard your footsteps on the stairs and felt you put your arms round my waist.''

Famous people who allegedly saw their own doubles or had their doubles seen by others include Johann Wolfgang von Goethe, Germany's greatest literary figure and estimated by some to have had one of history's greatest intellects. Goethe claimed that he saw his double or *doppelgaenger* ("double walker" in German) in 1771. That year, Goethe said, he had a vision of his future self while riding on horseback to Drusenheim.

Goethe wrote: "I saw myself coming to meet myself, on the same path, on horseback, but in a garment such as I had never worn... As soon as I had aroused myself from this dream, the vision entirely disappeared."

Eight years later, Goethe said, he suddenly realized he was on the same road wearing the garment "which I had dreamed about and which I now wore, not out of choice but by accident."

Roman Catholics have long believed that the doubles of saints and others have appeared to help the faithful, a process it calls "bilocation."

Perhaps the most famous case was in 1774 when a prisoner in Italy named Alphonse de Liguori became quiet in his cell and took no food for five days. When Liguori awoke, he claimed to have been at the deathbed of Pope Clement XIV. Liguori was said to have been witnessed in the pope's bedchamber.

In Scandinavian culture, appearances of the double are frequently so-called "arrival cases." In these cases, a person is tipped off that someone is on the way home or coming for a visit by first hearing noises made by the double.

In Norway, this noisy double is called the *vardogr* or "forerunner," and it makes the same series of sounds that the arriving person will later actually make physically. In the past, the appearance of the vardogr was so taken for granted, that people might commonly ask, on hearing the noises: "Is it you or your vardogr?"

On the borderline between doubles of the living and ghosts of the dead are the so-called "crisis apparitions" of parapsychology, which often involve a sick, dying or newly dead person appearing to a loved one at another location to announce the crisis. Sometimes, during the appearance, information is passed along to the percipient that he could not normally have obtained.

Belief in the existence of a spiritual double which could sometimes be seen has been widespread among ancient and native cultures. The ancient Egyptians spoke of the ka; Burmese Kaiens call the double the kelah, Melanesians have dubbed it the atai; the Wild River Shoshone of Wyoming call it the navujieip -- the astral projection of a medicine man's body wandering the earth and the spirit world.

3. The Voice...

In August 1992, Hurricane Andrew, packing 200 mile-per-hour winds, passed within a mile or two of Diana Garcia and Kelly Reeme, ripping apart their home, while they cowered in terror for hours behind a piano. At the climax of the storm -- as windows exploded and heavy furniture was sucked out of the shuddering house's gaping holes - a heavenly voice whispered to Kelly through the screeching din. What it said saved their lives.

Earlier that night, before the hurricane made landfall, the evening news had reported that their house was not in the evacuation zone. Diana, Kelly and a visiting relative, Ray, had gone to their rooms for the night with a false sense of security.

At 2:30 a.m., Kelly woke up suddenly. The house's sliding glass doors were rattling furiously. Kelly looked out the window: Palm trees were bending over in the wind. She turned on the TV. A newscaster happened to be saying, at that precise moment, that Hurricane Andrew had been upgraded to a Category 5 storm, the worst. And then, immediately, the power went out. It was a critical piece of warning news delivered to Kelly in a few fleeting seconds -- a small window of opportunity. Almost as if someone or something had wanted her to hear it. Later, she would never be able to pin down a broadcast at that time.

The storm is just starting, Kelly thought, awe-struck. If this is just the beginning....!

Despite Diana's protests, Kelly ran out headfirst into the rushing wind with Ray to the barn, opening the gates. Horses trotted out and disappeared into the night.

Ray came back wild-eyed and dripping wet. "It's really getting strong, Diana. I think we should be downstairs."

The three began to hear small flying objects pelting the house. *Clunk. Ping.* Above them, the roof was now creaking and heaving. Suddenly, its solar panels flew off. Then: An explosion inside an upstairs bathroom!

Kelly opened the violently shaking bathroom door, looked in. It was horrible. The skylight had been ripped out. Towels, the shower curtain, other articles -- all being sucked up through the hungry hole in the ceiling.

Kelly looked at Diana and Ray. Their faces were aghast. Now, she even felt herself being pulled into the room. She shut the door. It still rattled.

The three fled downstairs -- their ears now popping from the drastic change in air pressure. Tinkling glass everywhere.

Out of the corner of her eye, Kelly happened to notice a set of sliding glass doors buckling outward into a bow shape. Then -- the doors just peeled away and flew off into the night. Kelly froze, jaw dropping, shocked as she watched it.

"Kelly!" Ray shouted to snap her out of it.

The trio fled to the dining room, where another set of sliding glass doors now buckled and popped out, opening a gaping hole to the outside. Wind and rain invaded the room. The last vestige of light -- a candle -- was blown out.

In the inky darkness, the three overturned a dining room table as a shield from the darting debris now entering the exposed house. Three cowering rotweilers and a pet boxer, Daisy, wedged themselves among their masters be- hind the wooden table.

Suddenly, their shield was useless. A picture window in the nearby sunken living room burst out, allowing inside a torrent of new debris from a different angle. Ray screamed. He was bleeding. Something had hit him in the ribs.

"Let's go to the double doors," Diana shouted above the howling wind. Humans and canines, hunkered down or slinking, groped through the blackness toward two massive teak doors in a foyer. Objects whizzed by, impacting all

around them. Hard rain drove itself through the trembling house.

In the darkness of their new doorway shelter, Kelly felt the heads to be sure everyone, human and pet, was accounted for.

It didn't seem possible, but the screaming wind then got even louder. It sounded like a locomotive roaring through the house.

"Piano!" Kelly heard Diana shout. It was the heaviest piece of furniture in the family room. Better shield!

They got up, stumbled over rivulets of running water on the floor. Groping toward the family room, they held hands in a chain to brace each other and keep anyone from being blown out.

But Diana slipped. She fell. Bleeding from the glass-littered floor, she felt herself being forcefully sucked away from Kelly and Ray toward a huge hole in the living room -- where the sliding glass doors had been ripped out. Andrew wanted her outside, his first victim. Diana felt a firm hand clutch her bleeding leg. *It was Kelly!*

Somehow -- like a mother lifting a car to free her trapped infant -- Kelly mustered the super normal strength to raise Diana up bodily and throw her toward the piano. Ray, already there, grabbed Diana and jerked her down behind it into a fetal crouch. Kelly squeezed in alongside.

Now, even the massive piano itself, this Rock of Gibraltor, needed to be held in place by Kelly. The piano was trying to slide across the family room toward that hole in the wall. That massive Black Hole sucking everything into its event horizon -- and on to oblivion.

Andrew became more insistent in his search for the three. All the upstairs furniture was now being sucked out. Ray was praying. *"We're all going to die!"* he shouted. Kelly screamed into Ray's ear to be heard over the howling wind: *"We're not going to die!"*

The gusts ranged from horrible to indescribable. The frenzied wind whipped the rain in the house upside down so it fell toward the ceiling.

Kelly, shaking from cold and utter terror, felt heads. *Three dogs were gone!* Kelly hysterically screamed out the name of her favorite dog, her "child" -- one of the three missing. She felt her vocal chords vibrating but couldn't hear her voice in the din.

Dear God, she thought. "Please put your arm around me. I'm scared," Diana said to Kelly.

Silently, Kelly prayed St. Francis' serenity prayer....... And immediately, a strange, perfect calmness came over her. In the calm, she heard a supernatural voice. It spoke authoritatively to her: "Kelly, put your arm out!"

It was pitch dark. Kelly heard all sorts of potentially deadly projectiles rocketing around the piano. They ricocheted. They thudded off the walls. Stick my arm out? No way! Kelly thought.

"Kelly, put your arm out!" the voice repeated, more sternly. Kelly felt compelled to obey. Her outthrust hand was twisted into a backhand stance, sweeping the air up and down. Instantly, a two-foot-long sofa cushion shot through the foyer amid a shower of other debris. Kelly's hand snatched it like an intercepted football pass. She wrenched her arm -- and the cushion -- back inward to the piano. "Coincidentally," the cushion fit snugly between the piano and the wall behind her, plugging up an area that had exposed the three of them to debris.

Diana, however, was upset about it: Just one more wet thing! But virtually the exact moment Kelly put the cushion in place to shield them, she heard a loud pop: A two-story window in the foyer was ripped out, frame and all. Almost simultaneously, the sudden change in air pressure shattered the foyer's Versailles-like hall of mirrors into hundreds of sherds. Now, a tidal wave of glass -- tiny flecks and huge jagged spears -- shot down the hall. This deadly hail bombarded the piano's side, now shielded by the "coincidental" sofa cushion. For an eternal 30 seconds, the glassy torrent continued. Then it stopped. The sofa pad was a pin cushion, but there was not a scratch on Kelly. Andrew had been cheated once more.

"Put your arm out!" the voice commanded again. Instant obedience from Kelly this time. Her outstretched hand now felt a dog's head -- the "crazy" boxer Daisy, standing forlorn in the foyer. Kelly swept the pooch behind the shifting piano and into Diana's lap.

I wish the sun would come up! Kelly thought.

After two hours of blind agony, the winds slacked off at last just before dawn. Andrew was giving up.

Soon, Kelly, Diana and Ray could see a brightening greyness through the wrecked house's yawning holes.

"Ray, you got a cigarette?" an exhausted Kelly asked. But Ray's tobacco cache was a dripping mess.

In the growing light, the three saw a surreal world. Nothing in its place. Cabinet doors ripped away. Walls looking like dart boards or Swiss cheese, if they were not torn away entirely. Ex- cept for the piano, all the furniture had been sucked out of the family room.

Outside was worse. Ground zero of a nuclear blast. A rubble-strewn moonscape -- where at dusk the night before there had been beautiful gardens and neat fences. Not a leaf on a tree anywhere. Every palm tree felled. Grass brown, dead and discolored under a sullen blanket of clouds and windy drizzle. No living thing -- even insects gone. Diana's fax machine lay in the yard, split open like a boiled clam.

Miraculously, the missing dogs turned up okay; the cat, Kitty, was huddled intact inside a kitchen cabinet; and the ferret Casey was in the library.

Diana hobbled on a swollen foot and bleeding legs to a hand pump for water. Shivering from the cold, the three washed off the vomit and mud that covered their clothes. *They were alive!*

Within an hour, the clouds thinned out to a clear blue sky. Andrew's tantrum was over. Something beyond human understanding had kept him from getting his way.

"There's no way we can be convinced that there are no angels or some (such) force," Diana said simply.

3. Essay: The Otherworldly Voice and Clairaudience

Not too long ago, we learned by osmosis from our culture that people who hear telepathic voices need "professional" help. Yet, we now know this is largely untrue: It's fairly common for healthy people, and reports of it go far back in history. Socrates, the ancient Greek philosopher and the self-proclaimed "gadfly" of the Athenians, felt he continually heard the voice of a guardian spirit that warned him about things, although he said it never actually told him what to do.

Once, Socrates' never-erring spirit warned him against turning a corner. When his friends ignored the philosopher and went on their way, they were suddenly shaken up and knocked down by a group of pigs.

In parapsychology, the telepathic hearing of sounds or voices is called clairaudience (French: "clear hearing"). Prophets, celebrities, saints and mystics have heard these voices, identifying them variously as coming from angels, God, departed loved ones, and other sources.

In the Bible, the youngster Samuel, before he became a judge of Israel, heard the voice of Yahweh calling out to him, waking him up as he slept in the tabernacle sanctuary, and he thought mistakenly it was the priest Eli summoning him.

Joan of Arc, the French teen-ager who turned the tide of battle against the English during the medieval Hundred Years' War, insisted that she was given advice by angelic and saintly voices. No one can prove she was not deluded, but this much is clear: Joan was an ignorant peasant girl with no military upbringing, an adolescent who managed to take over command of the French army and lead it to one decisive victory after another. And she started winning her victories at a time when the English armies had been severely drubbing

France and had taken over much of the country in a long string of conquests. Joan was a woman who, in a highly sexist age, was acclaimed as a major country's top general.

Socrates and Joan notwithstanding -- in most cases, the telepathic voice does not come continually but rather sporadically. In fact, often it comes just once in a lifetime during a critical moment.

Commonly, the voice warns a person of danger or of someone else's need:

In 1951, Forest L. Wolverton of Snyder, N.Y. was snaking the family car along a winding West Virginia road on a Florida-bound vacation. A voice said: "Look out!"

Mrs. Wolverton snapped: "For heaven's sake, Forest, I'm in no mood for your jokes!" While Wolverton was protesting that he had said nothing, another voice screamed: "Look out!"

Wolverton checked the radio. It wasn't on. Mrs. Wolverton checked the glove department because their daughter Sally thought it was coming from there. Suddenly, both voices wailed together in concert: "Look out!"

The three Wolvertons were too shaken to continue. Wolverton pulled over onto the shoulder. Hardly had the car stopped, when another car shot around a blind curve in front of them at very high speed on the wrong side of the road. A head-on collision was barely avoided, according to Sally, who described the hair-raising incident in the December 1988 issue of *Fate*.

A friend of mine was once in a chicken house on a winter's day with his small son. Suddenly, a voice exclaimed: "Get out!" Instantly, he scooped the boy up and dashed out -- just in time to avoid the collapse of the building under the weight of heavy ice that had accumulated on the roof.

People who experience these things say that this clairaudience is often perceived as a telepathic "inner voice" but definitely is not a part of the person's own consciousness.

Sometimes, though, the voice is heard as an actual, physical sound clearly coming from the vicinity. In fact, in this case, the hearer often looks around to see "who" is talking and finds nobody.

Clairaudience, visions and the like are by no means rare in our time, as poll after poll shows. One example: In 1987, the Rev. Ben Johnson, a Lutheran minister with a Harvard doctorate, surveyed 14 Roman Catholic and Protestant congregations in St. Cloud, Minn. Two thousand people responded to the survey in that city of 45,000. Of those, 30 per cent claimed to have had an extraordinary experience, ranging from hearing heavenly voices or seeing religious visions to experiencing visitations or prophetic dreams.

In *A Man Called Peter,* Catherine Marshall tells how a supernatural voice saved the life of her famous evangelist husband Peter Marshall.

Marshall was walking home to the English village of Bamburgh across the moors under a very dark sky. Suddenly, he heard a voice cry urgently: "Peter!"

Marshall stopped, asked who it was, got no answer, shrugged it off and continued forward. "Peter!" the voice exclaimed again. Marshall stopped abruptly in his tracks -- so suddenly that he stumbled and fell on his knees. Jutting forward his arm to brace himself, he was surprised to find *empty space!* Marshall was on the very brink of a deep limestone quarry. One more step would have been fatal.

Traffic is a particularly common venue for the supernatural voice, which frequently is reported, for example, to warn a motorist to stop at an intersection despite a green light. A split-second later, another vehicle races out of a sidesteet and shoots illegally through the intersection.

Some of the people I've spoken with:

- A woman who was guided by a voice to a stranger's house where a man had just been stricken and needed emergency medical care.

- A motorist in the Washington D.C. area who was warned by a voice to change lanes -- just before a tractor-trailer topped a blind hill crest, headed the wrong way down the highway in the lane the motorist had just abandoned.

Whether the voice comes from the wisdom of the subconscious mind or an outside entity has been debated. Plato, the ancient Greek philosopher, felt that the voice comes from the divine part of a person's soul. By seeking wisdom and virtue, a person can strengthen his "voice," but a life of foolishness and vice weakens it, Plato argued.

Whatever the case may be, in the words of author Theodora Ward: "...Some men who are sensitive to the movements within their own inner depths find there a seemingly separate personality to whom they can turn for wisdom greater than their consciousness is capable of."

4. The Coincidence...

At exactly 7:27 p.m. March 1, 1950, three minutes before the beginning of choir practice -- a gas explosion blew apart the West Side Baptist Church in Beatrice, Nebraska. But not one of the normally punctual and well-attending choir members was there. They were kept away by a strange string of coincidences and -- they believe -- a divine hand.

Three days before the blast, there already was an early oddity: A visiting preacher, Dr. J.C. Gunst, told a Sunday night service: "What I would do if I were here with you folk. I would just push these walls out," Gunst said enthusiastically. But he was just talking about the need for the congregation to expand.

The following Wednesday afternoon, Rev. Walter Klempel, the West Side pastor, noticed that the sanctuary heated up unusually fast when he kindled a fire in the church's coal-fired basement furnace. What he didn't know: The rapid heating was due to large amounts of odorless natural gas that had accumulated in the church from a leaking pipe.

After warming the church for choir practice and services that Wednesday night, Klempel went home for supper.

Meanwhile, the temperature in the church continued to rise. At a sudden critical moment, the furnace's blower would come on. It would push the mass of highly flammable gas down into the basement where the open coal fire was burning...

Normally, Klempel and his wife would have been at church at 7 p.m., but their young daughter, Marilyn Ruth, had dirtied her dress, and Mrs. Klempel was ironing another.

"Is it time to go?" she asked. Klempel looked at his watch, not realizing that the normally accurate timepiece was unexplainably running five minutes slow that day. "No. We have time." They would be late.

Incredibly, so would each and every one of the other 15 persons expected there at 7:30 p.m. that night -- most of whom were usually early birds. Something that had never happened before:

- Teen-ager Royena Estes and her preteen sister Sadie got in the car to go to choir practice, but the car wouldn't crank. No problem: Charles Vandegrift, the father of fellow choir member Ladona Vandegrift, would take the Estes girls. However, 15-year- old Ladona was home, stuck on a homework geometry problem. She persisted with it, making herself late and also the Estes girls.

- Lathe operator Herb Kipf planned to be at practice early. But he was writing an important letter. He wanted to finish it before leaving home. It made him late.

- Mrs. Leonard Schuster ordinarily would have showed up at the church at 7:20 p.m. -- seven minutes before the blast -- with her small daughter Susan along. But tonight, she needed to go help her mother get ready to host a missionary society meeting.

- Machinist Harvey Ahl's wife was away from home. So a friend invited him and his two boys out to supper. Ahl got caught up in a mealtime conversation, lost track of time. He glanced at his watch. He, with his two sons along, would not be on time.

- Teen-ager Lucille Jones usually was punctual for practice. But for some reason, tonight she got interested in a 7 p.m. to 7:30 p.m. radio program, *This is Your Life*. She wanted to hear the very end of it. Her neighbor and fellow chorister, Dorothy Wood, came by as usual to walk with her to choir practice. Dorothy waited for Lucille, and both were late.

- Stenographer Joyce Black was in a lazy mood, lingering until the last possible minute in the warm house insulating her from the cold, blustery night outside with its biting wind. Lingering too long to be on time.

- Marilyn Paul, the choir's pianist, came home exhausted from work and dropped off to sleep in a rocking chair after supper. Marilyn's mother, Mrs. Fred E. Paul, the choir director for 14 years, tried to rouse Marilyn at first. But her husband suggested she let Marilyn sleep a little longer. As a result, both of the choir members, usually early, were late.

- Beverly Ellison, strapped with a difficult schedule of classes, decided to stay home that night and study.

Minutes before 7:30 p.m., the temperature in the traditional white frame steepled church was now high enough for the furnace blower to kick in. The invisible cloud of natural gas hovering under the sanctuary ceiling was sucked downward.

In the basement, this extremely flammable gas contacted the flames and heat of the burning coal fire. There was a colossal explosion in the basement -- right under the choir loft, where the choir members should have been -- and on every other Wednesday night always had been.

The blast blew out the church's walls sideways. It shot the roof into the air, which gravity then brought back down with a vengeance. The roof landed so hard, it drove the floor of the sanctuary down into the basement. The piano keyboard -- right beside where the choir should have been practicing -- was blown nearly a half block away.

The church was beheaded. Its steeple vaulted through the air and slammed into the middle of West Court Street, stopping traffic. As the steeple dropped, it downed a power line connecting Beatrice's radio station KWBE and its broadcast tower. The hands of the station clock froze at 7:27 p.m., fixing the exact time of the blow-up. The west side of town was blacked out.

- Marilyn Paul, up from her catnap, was putting on her coat to leave. There was a powerful bang. The whole house shook. Looking outside, she saw a blue flame shoot up among the treetops a block away.
- The Klempels were walking out when their power went off.
- Lucille Jones literally had just put her hand on the doorknob to exit when the bomb blew.
- Kipf was in a car ready to drive away. His mother ran out of the house: *"There's been an explosion!"*

A siren at the top of the Beatrice fire hall wailed for help. A dozen volunteer firefighters rushed from home.

Arriving at the church, fireman Joe Stiefvater saw a small fire flickering over a crazy quilt of tangled beams and warped collapsed walls in the 400 block of West Court.

The fire was easily put out. But the next task was infinitely harder: Digging through the rubble. *What are we going to find?*

Over the next 20 minutes, a miracle slowly unfolded. One by one, the different choir members ran up, at various times, to the rubble from different directions, each new arrival touching off a joyous round of hugging or kissing.

Around 20 minutes after the blast, Charles Vandegrift, his car filled with daughter Ladona and her young friends, Sadie and Royena Estes, heard the siren and saw barricades on the street.

"Wouldn't it be awful if it turned out to be the church?" he fretted. The Vandergrift car then disgorged its load of youth, putting the final wraps on the miracle:

"I can tell them to stop digging, because we're all here now," Kipf said, seeing the three young girls.

Awe-struck, the choir members spontaneously formed a circle on nearby LaSelle Street, holding hands to say thanks to the Architect of their deliverance.

In a universe which some say is ruled by blind chance, the West Side Baptist Church had discovered a clear sign of hidden will. But subtly expressed... in a slow watch, radio show, mealtime chat, geometry problem, school schedule, warm house, meeting, letter, and a nap.

Suddenly, the Beatrice area's previous claim to fame -- being the site of the first land claimed under the famous Homestead Act of 1862 -- was eclipsed. Life magazine did an immediate article, later excerpted in Reader's Digest. Even a TV crew from Japan, complete with interpreter, made the media pilgrimage to this town of 12,000.

As Ladona Vandegrift, now Ladona Steward, recently put it, "My thinking is that God said: 'It's not time for any of you. You've got more things to do. You have this story to tell for the next 50 years.'"

4. Essay: Synchronicity & Meaningful Coincidence

Is coincidence, as they say, God's way of working a miracle anonymously?

Writing in the January 1982 *Science Digest*, Robert Anton Wilson observed: "There have been coincidences so dramatic, so symbolic or so wildly improbable that they have aroused feelings of the uncanny in scientists and laymen alike for generations."

The world-famous Swiss psychiatrist Carl Jung noted that the world is filled with such "meaningful coincidences," both great and small. Mostly, we ignore these incidents, which Jung dubbed *synchronicities*. However, people who take an interest in synchronicities, even to the point of sometimes keeping diaries, often report that when they pay more attention to the coincidences in their lives, the coincidences multiply and intensify.

In some synchronicities, as in the Beatrice case, many see the hand of God or perhaps angels influencing things from behind the scenes:

- William Cowper, a famous British poet of the 1700s, once ordered a cab driver to take him to the Thames River, where he planned to drown himself. The cab driver got lost in a pea soup fog, wandered aimlessly around London, and finally confessed to Cowper that he could not even get the cab back to Cowper's home. Emerging from the cab, Cowper suddenly realized he was smack in front of his home -- after all that meandering. Cowper's response to the incident: Forgetting suicide, he instead composed a hymn still popular today: *God Moves in Mysterious Ways His Wonders to Perform.*

• During the Battle of the Bulge in World War II, the great wintertime German counter-offensive was critically threatening Allied troops in the Low Countries. German soldiers were taking advantage of continual snowfall, day after day, which kept the skies cloudy. This weather made useless the Allies' superior air power -- which was the Allies' great military advantage since the Luftwaffe had largely been destroyed. At that point, the flamboyant Gen. George Patton walked into a map room and began talking firmly with God. His staff looked on, startled. "I need four days of fine weather, Patton stated out loud to the Lord. "Otherwise, I cannot be held responsible for the consequences." Patton's prayer was distributed on 300,000 Christmas cards. Then, the skies, unexpectedly, did clear -- for the four days that Patton had requested. Allied warplanes took to the air, and the German offensive was broken.

Skeptics typically counter-attack that meaningful co-incidences -- even fantastic ones -- are inevitable statistical flukes. In his book *Incredible Coincidences*, Alan Vaughan reported how one speaker at the British Association for the Advancement of Science, declared: "If six monkeys were set before six typewriters, it would be a long time before they produced by mere chance the written books in the British Museum, but it would not be an infinitely long time." True enough, but Vaughan also noted that consciousness re-searcher Saul-Paul Sirag calculated that a randomly typing monkey would take 20 billion years -- the age of the universe to date -- just to accidentally type the phrase, "To be or not to be," at the beginning of Hamlet's famous speech in the Shakespeare play. To say nothing of the play itself -- or an entire library of books.

Psychiatrist Jung believed that meaningful coincidences are one of two connecting forces in nature. One of these connecting forces is obvious: cause-and-effect. Twist the faucet and, logically, water pours out.

But Jung said the other connecting force -- synchronicity -- brings together things that have no logical cause-and-effect connection but nonetheless share a common meaning. Like the elements of a dream -- all strung together illogically but still making perfect sense when you interpret the dream for its meaning. In this sense, a synchronicity would be like a waking dream. And it could be a meaningful symbol.

Consider the link between the presidencies of Abraham Lincoln and John F. Kennedy, so widely publicized after Kennedy was shot in 1963. Sure, there is nothing logical about linking the two presidencies. But look closer and a meaningful connection of sorts takes shape -- a symbolism. What follows is just the "tip of the iceberg" of one of the best known synchronicities (Described in more detail in *Seeing Your Future* and many other books):

- Lincoln and Kennedy were each elected president exactly a century apart, 1860 and 1960. Both were northerners promoting civil rights in a time of sectional tension between the states.

- Their vice presidents were both named Johnson (Lyndon and Andrew). Each vice-president was a southern Democrat and former senator. The two Johnsons were born exactly a century apart in 1808 and 1908.

- Both assassins were known by three-part names (Lee Harvey Oswald and John Wilkes Booth). The assassins were born exactly a century apart, 1839 and 1939.

- Both presidents were shot in the head, on a Friday, sitting beside their wives. Lincoln's assassin fired the shot in a theater and fled to a warehouse; Kennedy's assassin fired from a warehouse and then fled to a theater.

- Lincoln was shot in Ford's Theater. Kennedy was shot in a moving Ford convertible. The particular Ford model was a Lincoln.

The meaningful links go on and on.

Sometimes, synchronicities carry a deeply personal message for us -- much like a very significant dream. As in a dream, you have to interpret the symbols of the synchronicity to get the message. And as in a dream, it helps to be aware of what issues you are grappling with in your life at that time in order to interpret the coincidence.

For example, Jung wrote about a patient he once had who was an extreme rationalist (i.e., the physical is all there is; there is a "logical" mechanical explanation for everything, etc.). Progress was difficult. Then, one day, she told Jung about a dream in which she was given a golden scarab beetle. While the patient talked, Jung suddenly heard a tapping at his window. An insect was flying outside, banging against the glass. Jung raised the window and caught the bug in mid-air. It was a scarab-like beetle, the closest equivalent in Jung's area to the Egyptian insect the woman had just been describing. Jung handed the woman the bug, saying: "Here is your scarab."

This obvious synchronistic link between the inner mental world and the outer physical world broke down the woman's intellectual resistance to Jung's ideas and facilitated her treatment.

Indeed, when you are at a crossroads in life, contemplating big changes, synchronicities have a way of cropping up, bringing symbolic messages to you -- "signs," to put it coloquially.

Meaningful coincidence is even quickly becoming one of the most persuasive arguments for the existence of a hidden Creator -- in the so-called *Anthropic Principle:*

Scientists have discovered a multitude of freaky coincidences in nature which have worked together to bring about a universe suitable for intelligent human life. The force of gravity -- which could have had an infinite number of possible strengths -- happens to be just right, the strength of the force holding atomic nucleuses together is just right, the force of the explosive Big Bang was just right, the universe's age is just right, and so on.

And very often, had one or another of these forces varied by the minutest of degrees either way, a chain-reaction of ominous consequences would have been set off -- "fouling up" the evolution of the universe. These consequences would have led a universe in which intelligent human life could not have arisen, some scientists have concluded as a result of computer calculations.

To take just one of many examples, had the Big Bang's explosiveness deviated by an infinitesimal 1 part in 10 to the 60th power (1 followed by 60 zeros), a universe supportive of intelligent human life would not have developed, according to scientist Paul Davies.

In his 1983 book, *God and the New Physics*, Davies commented: "It is hard to resist the impression that the present structure of the universe, apparently so sensitive to minor alterations in the numbers, has been rather carefully thought out..." Davies adds: "...the seeming miraculous concurrence of numerical values that nature has assigned to her fundamental constants must remain the most compelling evidence for an element of cosmic design."

Indeed, to say that this incredibly fine-tuned universe got from the Big Bang all the way to us without a blueprint, by sheer accident, could be like saying that an explosion at an electronics factory could accidentally produce a mistake-proof functioning circuit board.

And like micro-universes, our own lives have been continually touched by "coincidences," mostly unnoticed, that -- added together over decades -- have decisively shaped our personal evolution, as if part of a hidden plan.

5. The Being of Light...

Three decades ago, as an 11-year-old preteen, Tami Kriens accidentally locked herself in her father's refrigerated meat truck, and there was no one to hear her screams for help. She banged on the stuck freezer door. She fidgeted with the unyielding lock. Shouted. Panicked. And finally, she gave up resisting death and simply prayed to be taken to heaven, a doomed child. Then, numbed by the intense cold, the Iowa farm girl watched in dull awe as brilliant beings of light appeared...

The days before her accidental entombment had been a series of blistering summer scorchers. On one of those days, she had walked past the open door of her father's truck and made a monumental discovery: As she went by, a current of deliciously cold air streamed over her hot skin.

Inside, Dad was taking inventory of the boxes of frozen steaks he delivered to restaurants. Like Columbus stepping ashore at Watling Island, Tami moved inside a New World -- the only air-conditioned spot for miles around.

"It feels really good in here!" Tami said. Her curious eyes swept the interior. Piles of boxed steaks.

Dad saw the open door. "We'll have to close the door to keep the steaks from thawing. Do you want to stay?"

What a question! The freezer quickly robbed Tami's body of its summer heat. She felt the intense cold. "How long would it take a person to freeze in here?" she asked.

"Within a short time, you'll be unconscious from hypothermia," her father said. After that, death.

Dad had on a thick, flannel shirt and a coat. He looked at his daughter, sporting only summer shorts and a light top. "You can't stay in here dressed like that."

Tami stepped back outside into Nebuchadnezzar's furnace.

Later on, though, Tami was inside again. Dad walked over to join her. "If you're going to go in there, you can't leave the door open," he said.

He showed Tami how to open the door from the inside: Push this bolt forward. Then twist the knob counterclockwise. Just like that. Tami watched casually. It seemed simple enough.

The following day, hour by advancing hour, the summer oven first warmed Iowa, then baked it, then broiled it. Humming fans blurred every window. Completely outclassed by the sun.

Again, Tami walked the 50 yards or so to Dad's freezer truck out by the garage. She stepped in and several minutes of delightful relief rolled by. Suddenly, she looked at the rear of the truck. The door was still open! Dad's warning flashed through her mind. Automatically, she shut the door -- a reflex without thought.

She cooled rapidly. Then, a sheepish feeling: Maybe I shouldn't be staying here. Time to go. She pushed the bolt forward, then twisted the knob and pushed. Nothing. The door wouldn't budge. Again, the push and the twist. Still nothing. And again... again... again... Panic stabbed her. She screamed.

"Mom!! Dad!! -- Help!! -- I can't get the door open!! -- Let me out!!"

Then, a horrifying thought: *Nobody can hear me!*

She ran from one end of the freezer to another, building up momentum and then slamming her shoulder against the door. She crashed a box against the bolt. She hit it with her fists. She stepped on a box to fidget with the bolt from a higher angle.

And, above it all, she screamed -- till she was hoarse. But the door was unmoved by her pleas. An Iron Curtain blocking the long life she was supposed to have ahead of her.

Twenty minutes went by. Tami, in shorts and a sleeveless top, was now light-headed, dazed by the cold.

She sat down, wracked by fear, and a warmth-hungry box robbed more heat from her legs. *I'm going to die!*

As far back as she could remember, Tami had believed in God. If she was doomed, at least God had the power to end her suffering now. She closed her eyes and raised her face upward: "Lord, I've done something very foolish. Please take me to heaven now."

The words of resignation were barely out of her mouth when she noticed a brilliant light. Immediately to her left and to her right were two dazzling figures of golden light. They towered upward to the ceiling. Inside each patch of light was the outline of an indistinct form. *The shapes were alive!*

Tami felt holiness coming from these Presences. And an overpowering love for her. *They're angels, and they care about me!* The angels picked Tami up and held her under the elbows. It was like two ushers escorting a wedding guest down the aisle: The trio -- two beings of light and an awestruck mortal girl -- glided toward the rear of the truck, where the door stood. Tami did not seem to be walking.

Were they taking her to heaven like she asked... *No, they weren't!* Tami watched the door open by itself. None of the three had touched it. The trio passed through to the outside.

Then, the angels vanished. Tami was left under the scorching sun. But it felt wonderful! A joyous mix of light, open space, and warmth.

Incredulity seeped into the exhilaration. Tami was stunned by it all. Still woozy, she walked slowly and carefully to her house. Tami was still too weak to mount the steps. So she sat down, leaning her head against a wall. Mother came by, laundry basket in tow, and brushed against her.

"You feel cold!" she said, startled. Later, Tami confided what had happened, though years went by before she revealed her story in public.

Claustrophobic screaming nightmares followed as her subconscious mind processed the horror of confinement. Nevertheless, Tami had also glimpsed the glory of a higher reality -- a few transcendent moments she chooses to remember now and then when the physical world occasionally becomes too dark and imprisoning.[1]

Tami's story originally appeared in different form in Joan Nyberg's A Rustling of Wings. Wingtip Press, St. Paul. $15.95

5. Essay: The Angel Seen as a Radiant, Superhuman Being

"I am well aware that many will say that no one can possibly speak with spirits and angels as long as he lives in the body... But by all this I am not deterred, for I have seen, I have heard, I have felt."
Emanuel Swedenborg

The intriguing "being of light" first came to the national eye during massive publicity in the mid-1970s about the "near-death experience" -- mystical visions people sometimes have of an alleged afterlife when they brush with death.

Researcher Raymond Moody, whose book *Life After Life* brought the NDE to the attention of the country, pointed out that one of the parts of a near-death experience is often an run-in with a brilliant "being of light."

What witnesses call this being -- God, Jesus, an angel, or something else -- varies according to their different religious beliefs. Secular people, for example, sometimes just use the no-strings-attached term "being of light."

But even though the naming of this entity is all over the place, the descriptions themselves are remarkably similar: This being is usually described as overwhelmingly loving and compassionate, profoundly wise, possessing a lively personality and even, some say, a sense of humor.

Its "body" is often described as a shapeless glow of dazzling light that nevertheless does not hurt the eye. In short, some sort of angel-like, benevolent superior entity.

You don't have to have a near-death experience to see a being of light. People sometimes encounter them -- and have other types of mystical visions -- when simply under great stress. Therefore, skeptics argue that what's really happening is just the mind snapping under pressure -- maybe pumping itself full of feel-good brain chemicals to bring on comforting hallucinations. (Or, as Ebenezer Scrooge told one of his ghosts: "You're just an undigested piece of beef.")

Believers, however, have at least two rebuttals:

First, stress can put people into an altered state of consciousness, which lets them sense other realities which normally aren't experienced in everyday waking consciousness.

Number two, these visions happen even when the perceiver is not frantic or strung out at all, but relaxed and centered. Consider this famous account from the Ballardvale, Mass. area, which occurred in the 1930s:

Smith College Professor Ralph Harlow said that he and his wife Marion were just out on a casual stroll along a wooded path of birches and maples, holding hands, when -- together -- they spotted six light beings floating overhead and conversing with one another, ignoring the Harlows.

After the vision faded, an astounded Harlow "compared notes" with his wife. They had identical descriptions of what they had each independently seen, said Harlow, a respected scholar sometimes solicited by attorneys for court testimony on more mundane matters.

In an article in the December 1986 *Guideposts*, Harlow quoted Episcopal Bishop Phillip Brooks: "This is what you are to hold fast to yourself -- the sympathy and companionship of unseen worlds. No doubt it is best for us now that they should be unseen. It cultivates in us that higher perception that we call 'faith.' But who can say that the time will not come when, even to those who live here upon earth, the unseen worlds shall no longer be unseen?"

Has that time come? Pollsters tell us that between eight and nine million Americans alone have had a near-death experience -- and this type of afterlife vision is just one of hundreds of different varieties of metaphysical visions.

Forty-six per cent of Americans believe they have a personal guardian angel and just under a third believe they have had experiences with their guardian spirit, according to a 1993 scientific poll reported in Time Magazine in conjunction with a cover story on angels.

All along, it turns out, the "unseen" has frequently been sighted, heard, felt or touched -- right under the noses of materialists who insist that the physical is all there is. But until recently, our materialist Western civilization kept these visions swept under the rug. Now, thanks to revealing polls, media publicity, and networking among experiencers themselves -- the genie is out of the bottle.

When a supernatural living light appears, it can take different forms. Some see the outline of a hazy human-like shape embedded in a brilliant aura. Others may witness shimmering columns of light. Sometimes just a general glow is seen.

I recall a particularly interesting talk show in Indianapolis where I took calls from people who felt they had had angelic or heavenly encounters. One man called in with the following story:

He had suffered severe back injuries in a fall and found himself in the hospital. X-ray results had doctors shaking their heads. He would be an invalid for life.

One night, he awoke in the middle of the night in his hospital room. He noticed that the room was suffused with a golden light. He sat up to get a better look -- then suddenly realized he was not supposed to be able to raise himself up in his crippled condition.

Next, he noticed a tingling sensation coursing from his head to his toes and back again, back and forth.

At that point, a nurse entered the room to check on him. She got an eyeful of the supernatural goings-on, screamed and ran back out.

The patient eventually fell asleep and on waking the next morning, he noticed that he was completely healed, walking around in his room with ease. He went to the nurse's station to find the nurse who had witnessed the healing. He was told she had quit her job.

6. The Near-death Experience...

Around mid-morning April 30, 1976, Sandi woke up fine, despite the nearly full bottle of sleeping pills she had swallowed hours before.

Even suicide wasn't working out right. Just add it to the list: A marriage in tatters, a miscarried baby, a dear one close to her who had recently been raped. That rape had dredged up horrible memories of her own sexual abuse as a child. To top it off, it was raining outside. Perfect symbolism.

Well, this time she'd do the job right. Sandi pulled a .32- caliber revolver out of a bedside table drawer, where her mother had kept it for security. A young nursing student, Sandi used the CPR two-finger technique to measure her chest and pinpoint the exact location of her heart. Overwhelming anxiety. Crushing sadness. Nobody needs me... I'm worthless... She put the barrel against her skin and pulled the trigger.

There was an instant thud in her chest. The ricocheting bullet pierced the heart's main artery, knocked off part of her liver and struck her backbone. But what a surprise! No pain.

But, then, a psychologically painful thought: Her mother would come home and find the sprawled body. *No!*

Sandi dialed for the operator, feeling woozy as internal bleeding began filling the cavity around her heart. "Here's a number to call the ambulance," the operator said.

"I don't think you understand. I just shot myself. Someone needs to pick up my body."

Suddenly comprehending, the operator was calm and steady. "Try to stay awake. And whatever you do, please don't hang up."

I wish she'd just let me pass out, Sandi thought groggily. And then, everything went black...

Next: There was a light in the corner of the room. A white translucent patch -- pulsating. More brilliant than anything she had ever seen. Sandi stared, transfixed. She saw the outline of a person's body, surrounded by a halo of hazy light. Rays of light fanned out from this halo in all directions. And golden flecks sparkled in the light.

A wave of love cascaded over her from this being -- a compassionate caring she had never felt from any human being. Also, a selflessness. A total understanding. And an utter peace.

She thought back to her childhood. Her Dad had told her once she didn't have to be scared at night because there was an angel in the corner of her ceiling. Was this an angel? And were those shooting rays what people had in mind when they talked about wings?

"Where did you come from?" Sandi thought.

"I've always been here. You just haven't been able to see me before," came the wordless, telepathic reply.

"She" -- the energy seemed to be female -- told Sandi to follow her. So Sandi thought "go" and her mere thought was movement.

The angel moved toward a huge, all-encompassing golden light. It dwarfed the angel's size. This larger light was also far brighter still than the angel's own staggering brilliance.

As Sandi looked, the angel merged into the ocean of greater light. The angel was absorbed. Sandi followed the angel inside and was also absorbed. She was still conscious of her own ego but, at the same time, she now shared an identity with this greater being.

Sandi sensed that this larger being was the life energy of everything in the universe. In a word, God.

Existential questions came to Sandi's mind. The unfairness, for example, of a universe in which billions are shoveled into hellish fires simply for not following this dogma or that doctrine. But the universe is not that way, the greater being replied. A person's condition in the afterlife actually depends on that person's inner spiritual condition. What is in a person's heart determines whether he is in heaven or hell. And judgment is a matter of the soul judging itself.

Why so many religions, conflicting ideas, so many things to divide us? Sandi asked.

These differences are challenges to look beyond the surface and see the truth that lies beneath, the Being said.

Sandi's life on earth up to that moment began to unfold before her -- like a grand movie. Every detail seen simultaneously. Every sense involved. She was both participant and viewer. It was like she had a million eyes or was accessing some multi-media super computer.

She even understood -- and felt -- what was going in peoples' heads and their hearts.

Sandi saw herself as a young girl in Augusta, Ga. raised by a financially struggling mother. Sometimes there was not enough to eat, and a black woman living nearby was feeding Sandi, happy to help the hungry child but worried about what racist neighbors might think.

"Why are some white people mean to black people? I think it's wrong," the child Sandi said.

"They don't know any better because that's the way they were taught, but God knows there isn't really any difference, and if people your age realize it's not right, it could make a difference," the woman said.

Now, bathed in this universal light, Sandi understood that the woman had been given hope by her visits. But Sandi also understood how the racism of that era had caused the black woman to mistrust white-dominated institutions, such as banks, hiding her money inside cracks in the walls of her house. A later scene flashed before Sandi: The woman's house was now being demolished and the money was being lost forever in the rubble, even though relatives could have used it.

In scene after scene, Sandi saw how the good and bad acts of people have a "ripple" effect -- how they set off a chain reaction of consequences, both positive and negative. No act was an act in isolation. No man was an island.

She saw a mentally retarded girl she baby-sat as a teenager. The girl had looked up to Sandi as her only friend. Yet Sandi's junior high classmates talked her into playing a trick on the girl, telling her that the school's football hero was planning to take her as his date to a costume party. During this life review, Sandi saw with great regret how this incident had made it hard for the girl to trust others afterward. Sandi felt the girl's disappointment, sense of betrayal and deep sadness. And she saw how this girl's new mistrust, in turn, caused others later to react negatively down the line.

Sandi also saw one of the worst things that had happened in her life: rape. She understood how rape was among the most terrible of crimes because it attacked the very spirit of a person, a horrible wound that would take tremendous love to heal. In some ways, it was worse than murder, which assaults only the physical body.

She saw how she had accepted a ride home from a man who then sexually attacked her -- and she now understood his twisted motivations -- revenge against other women in his life who had angered him.

Everything was interconnected. When we help or hurt others, we help or hurt ourselves, and set a chain reaction in motion.

As Sandi felt the pride or sorrow over her good acts and her mistakes, the greater being likewise felt the same emotions with her.

The life review began showing events leading up to her suicide.

"You can choose to stay here," the Being told Sandi. "But if you do, you'll have to go back to earth eventually and do it all over again." Relive all the hardships in order the learn the spiritual lessons enfolded in them. Sandi understood that her suicide, if successful, would be like dropping out of a course of study. It would have to be repeated before any credit could be given. No escape.

"If you do go back, you will get the family, the good mate and the love you're looking for," the Being said. A love Sandi had been craving all her life.

"It won't matter how you get the children, because these souls are destined to be with you," the being said cryptically, words she would only later understand.

The being also showed Sandi scenes of future events in her life. "You won't remember any of this until you need to," he said.

Among other things, Sandi understood that she would recover from her disastrous wounds if she returned.

Most of the knowledge she had received, in fact, would not be available to her in the physical body since her earthly form had not yet evolved to the point where it could handle it, the being said.

Sandi decided to go back. And instantly, the light faded. She was back in the bedroom where she shot herself -- amid a scene of hubbub and commotion. Paramedics were hurrying around. Suddenly, Sandi realized she was up above them, looking down on her body below. *She was out of her body!* And apparently she had been in spirit form since blacking out on the phone with the operator.

She watched the paramedics start an I.V., load her body onto a stretcher and slide it into an ambulance. *If I'm coming back, I need to stay with my body,* the disembodied Sandi thought to herself.

Such a fun feeling of freedom and lightness! She hovered outside the racing ambulance, sometimes passing through its outside walls to the interior to see her body.

At one point, her consciousness telescoped to another location. Two plainclothes police officers were arguing about her case. *They're wrong,* Sandi thought. They need to be corrected. Sandi moved among them, trying to straighten it out. They were oblivious to her.

Meanwhile, Kay, Sandi's sister, had awakened suddenly at the time of the shooting with one unexplainable thought: *Sandi is in trouble. We need to get to the hospital.*

Kay woke her husband.

At University Hospital, during resuscitation efforts, Sandi's spirit was sucked with a "swooshing sound" back into her body. Later, Sandi started popping in and out of her body during surgery.

On one "outing," she spotted a doctor talking in the hallway. "She's not expected to live," the M.D. told Sandi's stepfather.

Sandi also felt herself being pulled to the waiting room. There, she spotted the reason why: her mother, sister and brother-in-law were there, keeping a vigil.

Eventually, Sandi regained consciousness in her physical body. *Pain!* And one side of her body would not move.

"I want to go back," she announced. Back to the operating room? Why? the medical personnel wondered. But that was not what Sandi meant.

You won't walk again, even with braces, the doctors said. It's a miracle in fact that you made it through the surgery.

Why was Sandi so blase about her condition? they fretted. Was this a fatalistic surrender? Sandi didn't dare tell them that the reason she was unconcerned about her condition was that the greater being had assured her she would recover. A medical friend had tipped Sandi to stay mum about the journey to the afterworld. In the harsh materialist climate of the 1970s, there were legions of professionals ready to diagnose her as delusional if she were candid.

Sandi, wounded by life to the point of trying to escape it, had now returned to the "front" to do battle. Medical personnel remarked that she seemed to have an unusually strong temperament for a surviving suicide. Strangers came to her bedside to see the "miracle" patient who was not supposed to have lasted through the operation.

Sandi confounded the naysayers by learning to walk with braces, and eventually, even they, too, came off.

Gradually, her unglued life came together. Her string of bad marriages finally ended when she met Jack Rogers at an officer's club, the beginning of a happy 15-year marriage continuing today.

Eventually, after much prayer, Jack and Sandi adopted two children. And Sandi suddenly realized the meaning of the greater being's mysterious words: "It won't matter how you get the children because these souls are destined to be with you."

Today, Sandi asserts that suicide is a fruitless retreat: "It's pointless. You can't escape. You're going to have to go through it, anyway. You might as well stand your ground now rather than fight the battle all over again later. But (the experience) also lets me know that God doesn't give up on us."

6. Essay: Journey to the Brink of Heaven

"Life is a dream. When we die, we wake."
Mohammed

"In my Father's house are many mansions."
Jesus of Nazareth

"Someday you will read in the papers that D.L. Moody of East Northfield is dead. Don't you believe a word of it. At that moment, I shall be more alive than I am now. I shall have gone up higher, that is all -- out of this old clay tenement into a house that is immortal."
Evangelist D.L. Moody

"To die, to sleep; To sleep, perchance to dream: Ay, there's the rub..."
Hamlet

"Life is a great surprise. I do not see why death should not be an even greater one."
Vladimir Nabokov

"Nothing really matters except the answer to the burning question: "Am I going to live, or shall I vanish like a bubble? What is the aim and issue of all this strife and suffering?"
Malinowski

"I feel we are measured a great deal by what we do for others. That we're all put here to help one another... The greatest law we have is love."
An NDEer to near-death researcher Michael Sabom

Skeptics used to comfortably claim that otherworldly experiences are rare -- mostly the province of a lunatic fringe. It was a powerful weapon in the debunking arsenal. But in the mid-1970s, the doubting Thomases were suddenly disarmed -- at least on that point. Almost overnight, we discovered that millions of Americans believe they have glimpsed the after-life on brushing with death -- ordinary mainstream people talking about leaving their physical bodies, hovering in spirit form, glimpsing cities of light peopled by departed loved ones and other provocative claims.

In the early 1970s, death-and-dying expert Elizabeth Kuebler-Ross set the stage for this national upheaval by noting these alleged otherworldly journeys in her lectures. Then, in 1975, physician Raymond Moody published *Life After Life*, a runaway best seller with a startling message: People with different religious expectations about the afterlife -- or none at all -- were tending to experience the same types of afterlife visions when they came close to death.

This conformity was particularly strange, because the near-death experience was hardly known at that time.

Moody coined a term for these visions, which became an overnight household word: "the near death experience," or NDE, for short.

Suddenly, the floodgates opened up: Hundreds of experiencers "came out of the closet" to publicly tell their stories, on Sunday morning in church, to newspaper reporters over the phone, or just in coffee klatches with friends and relatives.

Pollsters went to work. One Gallup poll, for example, concluded that 1 in 20 Americans has had the experience.

Where in the world had they all been all this time? Mostly hunkered down, it turned out -- keeping quiet about it hitherto, for fear of ridicule in a materialistic culture.

"The NDE phenomenon has transformed quite ordinary people like housewives, mechanics and children into advocates for the reality of spiritual worlds..." wrote Richard Leviton in a *Quest* magazine article on the NDE.

In a complete NDE, a person typically reports leaving the body, journeying through a dark "tunnel," emerging into a higher world of light, and being greeted there by deceased loved ones, a religious figure, or a "being of light."

The description of the being of light is usually consistent: a shining angel-like superior entity -- a shapeless glow with a lively personality that is overwhelmingly loving and often concerned with helping the dying person evaluate his life on earth from a spiritual perspective. To that end, the dying mortal may view a three-dimensional, panoramic flashback of every tiny action in his earthly life -- trying to determine to what extent he had learned to develop within himself a spiritual love.

This spectacle -- the so-called "life review" -- is like a morality play, a technicolor theater-in-the-round in which not only one's earthly words and deeds are seen, but also one's thoughts and motives -- and how all this thinking and behavior affected other people spiritually, intellectually and emotionally, and finally, how these people, in turn, affected others as a result. A sort of moral ripple effect.

"Suddenly, my whole life began to unroll before me and I saw the purpose of it," wrote Leslie Grant Scott, quoted by psychic researcher Nandor Fodor. "All bitterness was wiped out, for I knew the meaning of every event and I saw its place in the pattern... I have never forgotten or lost the sense of essential justice and rightness of things."

How near-death experiencers identify this being of light -- which often oversees the "life review" -- depends on the individual's cultural background. Some might speak of seeing Jesus, some have called the being an angel or God himself. And some feel it is the higher self, the divine part of a person that stands outside of time and space. But whatever labels are used, the NDEers appear to be describing the same entity.

Near-death experiencers do not generally feel that their "judgment" (life review) experience was a matter of a hapless mortal weighed in the scales by a stern, unpitying God, inclined to sweep vast numbers of rejected "goats" into the flaming pits. Rather, they usually describe the judgment time as a team effort with a supportive being of light or as a self-evaluation -- all for the purpose of realizing spiritual growth.

In the world of light, the NDEer frequently runs up against some kind of figurative barrier beyond which the dying mortal may not trespass without dooming his chance to return to earth, so say the experiencers. A Texan, for example, told one researcher he saw a barbed-wire fence separating scraggly mesquite bush terrain (this life) from gorgeous pasture (symbolizing the afterlife).

During their adventures in the world of light, the NDEers often experience powerful feelings of joy and peace. They may even temporarily attain a higher state of awareness -- sometimes called "cosmic consciousness" -- particularly when they are interacting with a being of light. In this heightened awareness, the individual's consciousness merges with the universe, although the ego is not destroyed. The universe is understood to be an undivided gigantic loving organism intending good for all its interconnected parts. The self includes everything and everything is included with the self.

Richard Bucke, in his classic 1901 book *Cosmic Consciousness*, writes: "The man who goes through the experience knows that the cosmos is a living presence, that life is eternal, the soul of man immortal, that the foundation principle of the world is love and that the happiness of every individual in the long run is absolutely certain."

After they "come back," NDEers typically lose their fear of death, often develop psychic abilities, become less dogmatic in religious matters, yet more spiritual in their outlook. In *Otherworld Journeys*, Carol Zaleski quotes near-death experiencer Joe Geraci explaining how he tried afterward to hold on to the peaceful transcendent feelings of his NDE but was frustrated over and over.

"I couldn't watch television... Any type of violence, even an old Western movie, I'd have to turn it off..." Geraci said.

Rarely does anyone really want to come back. They've been in the penthouse and now, they must return to the basement apartment. Usually, they come back because they are told they have to or because they feel a strong attachment to loved ones left behind -- children to be raised, for example.

What effect is the NDE having on the rest of us -- the culture at large? The NDE and similar widely publicized spiritual experiences, like angel encounters, may be responsible for a growing belief in a spiritual world. Polls show such belief has been steadily inching upward. For example, a Time Magazine poll in December 1993 showed 69 per cent of Americans believing in angels. Other polls several months later showed the percentage creeping up into the low 70s.

In *Heading Toward Omega*, Connecticut psychologist Kenneth Ring suggests that NDE experiences may be advancing human evolution by radically changing the personal values and world views of millions of experiencers.

The NDE has helped humanize medical care of the dying, where a patient's visions are now more likely to be taken seriously. Not only are the near-death experiencers changed. Those who talk with them often are, too.

"No one who meets these people and hears their stories can come away without being profoundly stirred," commented Ring.

In the early 1990s, a popular theme of talk shows and newspaper articles was the criticism that the near-death experience is just too positive, "warm and fuzzy." What about the dark side of the force? the thinking went. It turns out that some experiencers, apparently a small minority, have had hellish and nightmarish experiences, although some have argued that these may be psychic nightmares welling up from the repressed areas of the subconscious mind at the point of death.

Also, some NDEers say they glimpsed, on their way to the world of light, a dark zone halfway between earth and the light-world -- jammed with huge numbers of grey, miserable spirits apparently clinging to our physical world. These descriptions are similar to the ideas of spiritualists that some souls are "earthbound" -- tied down to the physical plane by their own states of mind. Some are guilty, some angry, some deeply caring about something earthside, some insane or "shell-shocked" by violent deaths, some addicted to earthly vices.

As the Victorian poetess Emily Dickinson put it, "Who has not found the Heaven below, will fail of it above."

Still, the bulk of the reports are positive, though unpleasant NDEs may certainly be under reported. The average person -- who is neither Mother Theresa nor Genghis Khan -- seems to have a rather pleasant time of it during the NDE.

Suicide, however, reportedly tends to bring on either very unpleasant experiences or sometimes just conversations with beings of light warning that the attempted suicide was a serious mistake. As a result, near-death survivors almost unanimously feel that taking one's life is an error.

Some suicides report that their tormenting problems were merely transferred to the spirit world and if anything, instensified. Others say the sad scenes leading up to their suicide were played back, over and over again, without resolution.

Pediatrician Melvin Morse, who surveyed children's near-death experiences in *Closer to the Light*, reported how a seven-year-old, terribly abused by her parents, tried to kill herself by crashing her sled at high speed against a cement bench. The impact pushed her out of body, she said.

Soon, she was in the middle of a warm and loving bright light, which told her she'd have to return to physical life: "You have made a mistake. Your life is not yours to take." The child argued that no one cared about her. "You're right," the Light said. "Not one on this planet cares about you, including your parents." It was her job to care for herself, the being added.

When the girl returned to her seriously injured, painful body, she thought of trying suicide again but a sudden vision stopped her: She saw a nearby icy tree melted by a warm bubble, full of life, in which she saw herself. She saw that the melted tree would one day be green in the summer -- a symbol of how her loveless "wintry" life would eventually blossom. Later in life, she had children of her own and raised them with the love she had never had in childhood.

"Now, more than ever before," notes Atlanta cardiologist and NDE researcher Michael Sabom, "people are returning from the threshold of death" thanks to medical advances. "They are remembering more of their experiences, and we are listening."

And, as fellow researcher Kenneth Ring has suggested, these NDEers -- and others having had similarly deep spiritual experiences that transformed them -- may represent a new order of humanity with a greater awareness of universal spiritual truth.

Meanwhile, Paul of Tarsus advises: "The eye has not seen, nor has the ear heard... the things which God has prepared for those who love him."

7. The Physical Force...

All his life, Don Spann had had an unexplainable fear of drowning. Then, on April 25, 1993, Don came face to face with what had been haunting him so long -- when he was sailing a yacht off the Florida coast. A yacht that -- strangely but appropriately as it turned out -- was named *Perseverance*.

On that cloudy Sunday morning, Don's yacht was jarred by a powerful wave during a trip from Charleston to Fort Lauderdale. The shuddering boat catapulted the South Carolina industrialist off board.

Don was incredulous as he careened in mid-air, upside down, looking at the air between his inverted legs, heading straight for the Atlantic deep. As he splashed into the water, his outstretched hand managed to grab a steel rod on the edge of the boat.

He was dragged along in the boat's powerful wake. Don struggled to climb onto the boat despite the churning wake. It was impossible -- like sticking his head into Niagara Falls. His fingers ached.

A grim thought popped into his head. Between the wake and propeller, he could easily be injured, breaking an arm or suffering a cut. That would leave him unable to swim or as bleeding bait for the sharks. Better to let go of the rod.

Now adrift, Spann desperately waved, whistled and shouted. But helmsman John Thompson ("John T."), the only other hand aboard, could not hear him over the roar of the engine and its wake.

Gradually, the *Perseverance* dropped below the horizon -- with Don's life jacket on board. A few minutes later, the sound of its engines died away. Finally, even the dwindling bubbles of its wake were gone.

Spann was totally alone in the middle of the Atlantic -- a bobbing needle in a vast oceanic haystack, fighting for his life. Not even a shrieking gull was around to break the awful silence and solitude. He was a man overboard with less than a one per cent chance of ever being found and rescued in this type of situation.

At age 58, Don had toiled so hard -- usually a grinding seven days a week -- to build up his multi-million dollar business interests. Suddenly, it all seemed so pathetically irrelevant.

Mounting terror. Don scanned the watery lid of Davy Jones's Locker: a huge horizon-to-horizon expanse of undulating four-to-six-foot grey and black waves under sullen rain clouds.

Pleading, Don tried mental telepathy: *John T., turn around!*

A thick flock of rapid-fire prayers flew upward, like quail scattered by a hunter. *Please God, get him to turn around! God, if I have to die, let me at least die on land..."*

Don realized he had on a white T-shirt with colorful fluorescent stripes -- a beacon for passing sharks or swordfish-like marlins. The marlins were like cruise missiles, shooting at you from underwater and impaling you in a surprise attack.

But with sharks, it would be worse. First, they would partially surface -- their fins circling the prey. *Oh, no...* He was gasping for air, hyperventilating. To stave off panic, which would drown him, Don mechanically recited his personal motto: "Convert unknowns to knowns... Convert unknowns to knowns... Convert unknowns to knowns...

He started thinking. It held down the fear. *Can I swim to safety?* The Daytona, Fla. shoreline was 20 miles away to the west. But much longer, actually, since he'd be swimming with the current, moving diagonally along. He'd have no chance to get there. *Besides, you never leave the scene,* he thought, remembering his Marine training.

Convert unknowns to knowns... Your best chance is to stay put and face yourself in the direction that the boat left in case it comes back. Use the rain-swollen clouds and a break in the sky as landmarks to keep you oriented to the *Perseverance's* path. John T. will definitely come back. *But will I still be alive?*

The cold water -- 67 degrees -- steadily sucked heat from Don's body. He could slow the onset of hypothermia by moving around. But don't move too much -- conserve energy. Avoid cramping.

Don did a breast stroke with a scissors kick, carefully keeping his hands underwater so as not to make a splash which would attract curious little fish, who in turn, might attract something bigger and more deadly, making Don part of the food chain.

At the helm of the *Perseverance*, John T. looked around. Where was Don?

In horror, John T. checked every nook of the yacht, including some spots almost impossibly small. *He's overboard!*

John T. began flawlessly performing a series of rescue procedures, including a critical Williamson Turn, a precise way of turning the boat around and back to the exact position it had been sailing from. Few sailing students remember it, but "coincidentally" the 25-year-old college senior did.

Don's life depended on that turn being executed correctly and on dozens of other things that John T. next did correctly and expertly. John T. grabbed the binoculars and remembered how to methodically sweep the horizons for a man overboard -- not piecemeal. He remembered to pull back the canvas and mount the boat's highest spot.

But the *Perseverance* had already gone about eight miles, a terrible distance for a successful recovery on the open sea. John radioed the Coast Guard: *May Day*. It was the worst day of his life...

Don's muscles were numb. His neck ached horribly from continually arching his head backward. He flipped over from a prone breast stroke to swimming on his back to rest. Then another flip. And another. *I am so tired.*

Don's mind suddenly "stopped" -- and he heard a malignant negative voice: "Why don't you just give up and slide on down. It won't hurt." It seemed to make sense, Don thought. Why not? Then, something clicked in his mind. *No!*

"I'm going to fight," Don said.

"John T. is not going to come back," the voice said angrily.

Now, Don himself was angry. That was a lie. John T. would come back. Don looked up at the empty air: *"I'm going to swim all day and all night. You got that!!"* The voice went away.

The minutes ticked by... Then, 45 minutes after he first hit the water, as Don was undulating on his back kicking with his burning leg muscles, he heard a distant thrumming... It grew louder. *An engine!!!* His heart soared.

Don flipped over on his stomach to look. But the watery horizon was featureless. *Oh, no, I'm hallucinating.* His heart shrank and plunged.

No. There's the sound again. That was *Perseverance's* engine! Wait, don't roll over yet for another look. You only have the strength to do it once. Don paused until the engine was louder than ever. Flop.

Don was on his stomach. He could see the 46-foot yacht! A far-off tiny sliver. What's this? The yacht was not coming straight on, but at an angle -- from 12 O'Clock to 9 O'clock. *He's got to come closer or he'll never see me. God, please don't let him go by and disappear in the other direction!*

Gliding diagonally vis-a-vis Don, the *Perseverance* was at 11 O'Clock, 10:30, 10, 9:30... Don could see the distant figure of John T., very systematically sweeping the horizon with field glasses -- but sailing right on by!

The lenses of the glasses passed over Don. The binoculars moved on.

Suddenly, the little figure of John T. froze and the binocs snapped backward -- looked directly at Don.

"Don!!" John T. shouted.

Oh, thank God, he sees me! Desperate to rest from the breast stroke, Don forced his tortured muscles to roll him over onto his back, and he momentarily passed out. He was almost finished.

The *Perseverance* began backing up. An equally dangerous time was now beginning. Many men overboard are actually lost at the very point of rescue.

John T. shouted: "Don, look at me! I'm going to throw you a line!"

"Hit me the first time. I can't swim!" Don gasped.

A 50-foot nylon rope snaked out from the boat over the water. Typical of the uncanny precision with which John T. had done dozens of critical things during the crisis, the rope made a direct hit on the first toss, smacking Don on his bald spot! But it felt like a pure million dollars.

Don was too weak now to grab and hold it, so he limply wound the rope around his hand. John T. tugged on the rope, pulling Don toward the boat's swimming platform.

As John T. lowered the boarding ladder, the yacht jumped in the waves, and the swimming platform pushed Don underwater! *Move!* Don pleaded with his muscles in the underwater blur. It's only 10 to 20 feet to the ladder. But his limbs were paralyzed, their last ounce of energy spent.

Don noticed a soft diffuse light -- tints of yellow, green and tan, above the water line. Then, a thought distracted him from that strange light: *Don, you've been underwater for a while now, why aren't you hurting for air?*

Splash! Displaced water streamed against Don, and he was surrounded by air bubbles. What? Oh: John T. jumped in! But that's not smart. But wait, he probably tied himself to the boat first.

Don relaxed and thought: Don't fight him. Don't struggle.

Suddenly, four firm hands clamped themselves around Don's upper and lower arms, two on each side. Don was startled. Who else is in here?

As he floated limply, Don next felt hands pressing against him from the back, propelling him rapidly toward the boat. At least two, possibly three people. Another shock: he was vertical. How could be moving that fast in a vertical position?

The boat's chrome ladder loomed up in front of him. Don tried, but his leg would not lift itself onto the rung. Then, Don felt the fingers and thumb of a hand grab his calf and another hand cup itself under his heel. The two hands pushed the leg onto the bottom rung of the ladder. Then, two hands shoved his body up-ward.

Standing on board the *Perseverance*, John T. saw Don's head pop out of the water. Adrenalin powered John T.'s 120-pound frame as he hauled his 190-pound skipper to safety.

Don, suddenly gasping for air and beginning to shake uncontrollably from hypothermia, dropped like a dead weight.

Things moved fast. In a few minutes, a helicopter chopping the air lowered a basket to haul Don up for evacuation to University Hospital in Jacksonville, Fla.

At the hospital, John T. finally arrived. The two friends embraced.

"You have the biggest, deepest thanks I know how to give to anybody," Don said. "You know, you scared me half to death when you jumped in the water," Don said. "You and your friends saved my life, pushing me to the boat."

John T. did not have a look of understanding. "What do you mean? Don, I never left that boat. There was nobody in the water with you. You were alone. You got yourself to the boat."

Don was thunderstruck. A wave of emotions choked off his voice. *God answered my prayers. My guardian angels were in the water.*

During 11 hours in an emergency room, Don had plenty of time to think: Okay, God. You've got my attention now. What are you trying to tell me?

The same answer kept coming: I'm a workaholic.

Life -- like John T. and the *Perseverance* -- was threatening to pass him by. The proverbial roses were going unsmelled.

Don's wife, B.J., came in. After crying together for a while, Don wiped his eyes and spoke: "I keep coming back to this thought about why this happened." "I know why," B.J. said. "How can you? I haven't told you." "Take time to smell the roses," she said.

7. Essay: Physical Intervention

> How did he git thar? Angels.
> He could never have walked in that storm.
> They jest scooped down and toted him
> To whar it was safe and warm.
> And I think that saving a little child,
> And fotching him to his own,
> Is a derned sight better business
> Than loafing around the Throne.
> **John Hay's Little Breeches**

Spiritual experiences run along a continuum -- from the very subtle to the earth-shattering.

On the mundane end of the spectrum are the meaningful coincidences that all of us sense at times and that occasionally rattle the cold logical mind. You accidentally step off the subway train at the wrong station and bump into a long-lost lonely friend waiting at the platform for another train.

Ratcheting things up a notch, there are the vague feelings, emotional hunches and premonitions -- also widespread. On a feeling level, evangelist Billy Graham was so worried about President Kennedy's safety in Dallas that he tried to contact him to warn against any trip there, but could not get through.

At the high "dramatic" end of the continuum are the somewhat less common telepathic voices -- warning motorists, comforting a terrified soldier on the battlefield...

Further on down the line, the full-blown visions: Salvation Army founder General William Booth seeing angels cloaked in brilliant, rainbow light.

And finally: physical intervention itself is reported. The angel wrestling with Jacob. Spirit manipulating matter.

To borrow a phrase from the singer Olivia Newton-John, but in another context: Angels do sometimes "get physical." Or as writer Tobias Palmer put it: "Angels can be very strong and tough in their service to us. They often challenge us and confound us and startle us and even knock us about... They pound upon our lives when our lives have gone to sleep."

In this physical intervention, we may get something as dramatic as a shove, a yank, a supporting hand when we falter, or even the lifting of a vehicle from one dangerous place to be set down at another, safe location -- according to those who have seen this phenomenon first-hand.

Hans Moolenburgh, a Dutch surgeon who caused a media stir in Holland when he asked 400 surgical patients at random if they had ever seen an angel and was told "yes" by eight per cent of them, came across this case:

A Dutch woman told Moolenburgh that, as a young girl riding a bike in Limburg, she was accosted by a military truck full of whistling and waving German soldiers during the Nazi blitzkrieg invasion of Holland in 1940.

She angrily turned her face away from the invaders. The driver of the truck, apparently seeking revenge, then swerved the vehicle and bore down on the bike to run her over. At that point, a supernatural force, she said, picked up the bike and transported it through mid-air to another, safe spot, setting it down again. Another cyclist pedaled up to her, saying he had seen the levitation and asked in astonishment how it could have happened, Moolenburgh reported.

Angels seem to get "hands on" the problem particularly often in traffic. An invisible hand may grab a pedestrian and pull her out of the path of an oncoming truck; seize the steering wheel and veer a car off a collision course with a hitchhiker hidden by fog; paralyze the accelerator to keep a car stationery at a green light seconds before another car, violating the right of way, shoots into the intersection illegally against a red signal. Then, after the danger is passed, suddenly the accelerator is working again. Typical scenarios.

Dinah Arnett, a Tampa, Fla. businesswoman, was driving on Interstate 4 near Disney World in the early 1980s. Suddenly, she said, an unseen force grabbed her steering wheel and forced her car off the interstate, down an exit ramp and onto State Road 27. From there, the automobile continued driving itself until it pulled into a service station lot. The car finally parked itself right in front of a service bay.

At that point, control of the car was returned to Dinah. She exited the car, and a few seconds later, she said, the right front tire exploded. She interpreted the whole incident to mean that her late husband, who she feels is her spiritual guardian, had known a dangerous blow-out was about to occur at high speed on the interstate and had taken matters into his own hands to prevent that from happening.

There is also a class of stories in which motorists insist that they somehow missed colliding in a narrow space where two cars could not have passed each another. Yet neither car was moved out of the way.

For example, in the 1930s, William E. Clark and a carload of fellow football players met an oncoming pickup truck on an impossibly narrow bridge, Clark reported in the summer 1989 *Spiritual Frontiers*. They braced for a horrible collision, but experienced only a "blur of motion" and then saw the pickup moving off behind them. Clark's football coach and other players in the vicinity witnessed the baffling incident in broad daylight. In fact, one of the youths and his father went so far as to measure the bridge's width.

In one type of physical intervention story, someone is stopped by an invisible barrier that will not let him go on -- like one of those force fields in Star Trek. Rodney Kephart, a North Dakota veteran, says an angel saved his life during World War II by keeping him from going into an empty Wake Island hospital room to sleep when he went off duty. After being rebuffed three times when he tried to enter the room, he finally walked a quarter mile to his regular bunk.

Shortly thereafter, during a Japanese attack, an incendiary bomb struck the very hospital room Kephart had tried unsuccessfully to enter. The bomb touched off a fire that destroyed the hospital.

Sometimes, when we don't have the strength -- literally -- to meet a situation, a physical force moves in to bolster our inadequate muscles:

Pennsylvania retiree Elizabeth Large recalls how, as a young child in the late 1930s, she became trapped inside a junked refrigerator while playing hide-and-seek. As she banged on the door and became desperate, thinking *"I'm going to die because I can't breathe"* -- she heard a telepathic voice say: *"Push on the top."*

As the little girl began pushing, it seemed to her as if somebody else took over her arms, giving her super strengh. The flat top of the refrigerator came off, and she crawled out.

After escaping, Elizabeth thought she'd better put the lid back on the refrigerator or her father might be angry. The six-year- old then tried to pick up the lid, but it was now too heavy for her to even lift up one corner.

Although the idea of non-physical angels or mental energies moving things around may seem startling, something very much like this has been known to parapsychology for decades: Psychokinesis, the alleged use of mind-force to move objects.

In the late 1960s, the brilliant physicist Helmut Schmidt made waves in scientific circles with a rigorous experiment that tested the mind-over-matter idea. He built an electronic "coin flipper." The machine had a panel of nine lamps arranged in a circle. Unpredictable radioactive decay made "heads" or "tails" come up totally at random. And that, in turn, decided whether the panel's lights would flash clockwise or counter-clockwise. Test subjects tried to use mind power to will the lights to move in one direction only. The results of 15 subjects achieved odds of 1,000 to one against chance. Eventually, Schmidt's highly regarded experiment was written up in conservative scientific publications.

8. The Moment of Death...

When Scott Degenhardt turned 18, his mother gave him a set of suitcases for his birthday. More than a hint.

It was the final stage in the breakup of his family. His father -- an duty bound assistant prosecutor struggling with workaholism, heavy drinking, and steep debts from an earlier failed business when he refused to file bankruptcy -- had already moved away. Divorce papers later made it final.

Scott, rebellious, estranged from his parents, searching for something, was soon living on the streets, sleeping in his car or in the dining area of a fast-food place, taking birdbaths in rest-room sinks.

Looking for something to fill the inner and outer voids, the one-time atheist teen now fell in with different fundamentalist cults. Hand over all your money to us, one group said, and God will take care of your payments on your jeep and your student loan. Rather than worry about worldly things, he could better spend his time passing out save-your-soul pamphlets on the street corner.

The brainwashing was deep. Scott's thoughts became a mirror of their thoughts -- almost. Something deep within still twitched with unease at how the group forced people to believe and grubbed for money.

When the group broke up, Scott again escaped the streets by casting in with Brother Bryant (pseudonym), a hard-core Biblical literalist and tent revival preacher. Bryant had a scriptural reason to forbid virtually everything under the sun -- including laughter and comedy, and even Scott's favorite pair of overalls, which he was forced to give up for more suitable attire.

Brother Bryant was stout and red-faced as he yelled out sermons and gestured over dramatically. In his own way,

Brother Bryant was, surprisingly, a good speaker. And the music was good. He actually had a good show.

Out of the pulpit, he wore an eternal pasty, artificial look on his face.

The money came in by the hundreds of dollars a night. Bryant liked to keep it in a thick wad of bank notes which he was fond of flashing. Little of the mammon, however, filtered down to his disciples pitching and striking the big tent. While Bryant dined on steak, they dug into peanut butter and jelly sandwiches.

Meanwhile, as Scott joined Brother Bryant on an interstate crusade, God was definitely not taking care of Scott's debts, around $5,000 in all that his newly divorced and financially struggling parents had co-signed for.

One day, a letter came from his father with news that hit Scott like a lightning bolt. On Valentine's Day, the day he was born, Ronald T. Degenhardt had doubled over with pain. The first diagnosis, gall stones, was soon changed to highly virulent esophageal cancer. A liver scan left little hope: The cancer had already spread to every major organ and was inoperable.

"I would like to be closer to you..." the letter said.

Ron had never really had a relationship to speak of with his son. No bonding. Never an "I love you" or an embrace. Ron's life had been chaotic. A stressful job, debts, alcohol, strained relationships. Had Scott been the final straw that sent his father's immune system into a tailspin? The thought stabbed the youth.

Scott also thought of his growing disenchantment with Brother Bryant, who was growing more and more extremist, if that were possible. Lately, he'd gotten a number of the crusaders arrested in a conflict with local authorities.

Dad's letter was the final straw. "I'm going home," Scott told Brother Bryant. Brother Bryant immediately went to work on Scott: If he took off, he'd ruin his life! Be a failure.

And probably end up in the hot, licking flames of eternal perdition!

Scott was beyond manipulation.

Brother Bryant then broke his promise to pay Scott's fare home if he had ever wanted to leave -- for Scott's own good, of course. When he saw Scott walking off anyway, however, the preacher did concede him a $10 bill for the three-state trip.

That night, Scott walked 36 miles along a desolate highway leading to the interstate. Then, he was nearly killed when he hitchhiked with a driver who turned out to be intoxicated and sideswiped another vehicle -- and then another driver who suddenly accelerated to 90 miles an hour and started passing cars on the shoulder and median. Luckily, the drunkard had to stop for gas and Scott bailed out.

Later, it was hard to talk with ordinary people. "I was a fundamentalist robot," Scott recalled. Brother Bryant had earlier convinced Scott to disown his family and avoid normal topics of conversation as "secular and worldly" -- even popular music on the radio. Scott began de-programming himself.

Scott immediately noticed a striking change when he met his father. Ron, who could never express his emotions, now showed them freely. He exuded a spirituality and a heightened awareness that had been missing -- as if a light had been turned on.

For the next two months, the 20-year-old Scott got to know his father for the first time in his life. They ate lunch together, shared their feelings.

His father also mentioned a mysterious recurring dream he was having: A man walked in the background, holding up a sign with the number 30.

By the time the end approached -- as hospital personnel were constantly draining fluid out of Ron's lungs while family members and even nurses stood by crying -- the healing of the father-son relationship was complete. The strong-willed Ron, maintaining a stiff upper lip to the last moment of consciousness, slipped into a coma.

"I love you," Scott told his unconscious father. "And I appreciate how you showed me the value of honesty and hard work."

Now, there was nothing to do but wait for the call.

Around 10 p.m. on May 29, Scott lay down in bed, aching from sadness over the loss that was to come, but at peace, too. He was getting a new start in life, but his father would never get to see what he would become, never see his future wife and children...

After about an hour, Scott drifted off to sleep.

Suddenly, sometime later, Scott abruptly awoke. A whitish vapor was shooting toward him from the foot of his bed. The cloud stopped. It hovered in the air over Scott's left shoulder as he sat up in bed. *Dad!*

It was Ron from the waist up, but looking about 10 years younger than his age, 45. He smiled. His body was misty, with a see-through translucence.

Like a tidal wave, Scott was hit telepathically with a mass of emotions and thoughts from his father. It was like being in his father's head -- and in his heart. An ecstasy at being free not just from the pain of cancer but from the very physical body itself. A genie free of the bottle.

How does it feel to be out of your body? Scott asked, later realizing the foolishness of the question, since he was completely sharing his father's thoughts and feelings. Ron answered by throwing more of the joyful feelings into Scott's mind. *Exhilarating, but that word doesn't really convey it,* Ron's mind said to Scott's.

Scott was so happy for his father. It seemed so right.

The youth and his father both seemed to be in a higher state of consciousness, where mental activity was much quicker than in physi cal existence. The question-and-answer back-and-forth soon escalated into a rapid-fire swapping of emotions and thoughts -- how Scott felt for his father and how much his father loved him.

Gradually, Scott began to take notice of his surroundings. The thought came to him: Is this real or a dream? Look around the room and see if everything looks normal. Scott looked down. *He saw himself!* His body was lying on the bed, eyes shut, asleep. He was half out of his physical body, sitting up in his spiritual body.

Scott could see where his spiritual torso rose up out of his physical body. He looked at his spiritual hands and arms: misty and translucent like his father's form. Terror iced its way through Scott. He didn't know anything about out-of-body experiences of the living. *Does this mean I'm dead, too, like Dad? And if I'm not, how am I ever going to get back in my body?*

Scott also heard an uncomfortable buzzing sound, which he would later learn is the first stage of a near-death experience.

As Scott continued to look around his room, he noticed that he could "see" wherever he directed his attention, even if he didn't face the object with his spiritual form. I'll try looking at everything in the room at once, he thought. *It worked.*

Scott calmed himself and looked toward his father. He was still there. Calm down, Scott thought. You might as well enjoy this experience. This is probably the last time you'll see Dad. Scott felt a connection re-establish itself between him and his father. They basked again in each other's presence.

Eventually, though, he sensed another connection opening up -- between the two of them and... infinity. Coming from the other link, Scott heard the voices of different beings, speaking indistinctly among themselves -- higher spiritual beings overseeing the situation, Scott intuited.

One of them said something to Ron, who looked in the direction of the new opening. "They're calling me now. I have to go," Ron said.

"Great!" Scott replied jubilantly.

Ron's spiritual form swooshed off in the direction of the opening. *I can follow him there, if I want,* Scott suddenly realized. But as soon as the thought crystallized in his mind, Scott received a thought from outside himself: *It would not be proper for you to do that. It's not your time yet.*

Then, the connection closed up. Scott lost consciousness. The next thing he knew he was sleeping, awakened by the ringing of the telephone. Scott's mother got to the phone first in her room, then came to Scott's room.

I know what she's going to say but let her say it, Scott thought to himself. "It was the hospital," she said. "Your father has died."

"I know."

"How do you know that?"

"He was just here. I was talking with him."

The time of death was 12:15 a.m. May 30. Scott thought about his father's recurring dream of the man with the placard marked with the number "30."

The afterglow and elation of Scott's mystical experience kept him "supercharged" for weeks afterward.

"There was never the slightest doubt that I was out of my body and saw my Dad. There is a difference. When you're out of your body, thinking is much faster and clearer than even on your good days, and your senses are much sharper. Things are so readily understood that it's hard to misunderstand," Scott says.

At the funeral, Scott surprised himself by almost bursting into laughter as he came up to the casket for the viewing. Amid all the gloom and crying around him, Scott saw Ron's pale, groomed body for what it was -- just an empty shell, a cast-off garment. *Scott knew.* He had been there himself.

"We do resurrect after we die. We do have a better life waiting for us. It is far better than we can imagine," Scott says.

8. Deathbed Visions and Moment-of-Death Experiences

"Because I could not stop for Death/ He kindly stopped for me/The carriage held but just ourselves/ And Immortality"
Emily Dickinson

"Swing low, sweet chariot. Coming for to carry me home..."
Spiritual

"Dying is a wild night and a new road,"
Emily Dickinson

"It is as natural to die as it is to be born."
Lord Bacon

The moment of death often temporarily parts the heavy curtain that shrouds the next world from this one. Consider these points:

Psychic -- particularly telekinetic -- activity may accompany it, such as clocks stopping, pictures falling, or kitchenware breaking. For example, at the moment inventor Thomas A. Edison died, the clocks of two of his associates suddenly stopped. Just a few minutes before that, Edison's own grandfather clock stopped.

Like midwives in reverse, heavenly beings are often said to show up at the deathbed to help the dying exit this world into the afterlife. The dying may have visions of dead loved ones, angel-like beings of light, or religious figures like Jesus, the Virgin Mary or, for instance, in India, Yama, the Hindu judge of the newly dead.

Because the dying say these entities are coming to escort them into the next world, they are called "take-away apparitions" in parapsychology. To the ancient Greeks, these figures were known as *psychopompoi,* escorters of the dying soul.

Indeed, a person about to die may suddenly perk up and start speaking excitedly and animatedly with something or someone invisible to onlookers in the room. After the strange conversation is over, death usually follows immediately or shortly thereafter.

Just before he passed on, the famous American evangelist Dwight L. Moody murmured: "Earth recedes. Heaven opens up before me. I have been beyond the gates. God is calling. Don't call me back. It is beautiful. It is like a trance. If this is death, it is sweet."

Moody's face suddenly lit up. "Dwight! Irene! I see the children's faces." (Two of Moody's small grandchildren had earlier died.) Moody turned to his wife: "Momma, you've been a good wife to me..." And then, he lost consciousness. The entire incident is recounted by Moody's son in a biography of his father.

Cases with children are particularly touching. Herbert Greenhouse cites a typical example in the death of a 10-year-old orphan reported in Baird's *A Casebook for Survival.* The child and a medical officer saw a luminous globe descend on the youngster, lighting its face.

"Oh, Mama, Mama, I see the way, and it is all bright and shining." The light rose, and the child died. This story also points up the fact that occasionally someone besides the patient reports seeing the take-away apparition or perhaps only a mist of energy rising from the newly dead physical body, as happened with the famous *Little Women* author Louisa May Alcott.

Alcott described the death of her sister Betty this way: "I will tell it here, for Dr. G. said it was a fact. A few moments after the last breath came... I saw a light mist rise from her body and float up and vanish in the air. Mother's eyes followed mine, and when I said, "What did you see? -- she described the same light mist. Dr. G. said it was life departing visibly."

But even in cases where nobody witnesses the vision except the dying patient, the onlookers are often deeply impressed.

"Chill after chill went down my spine," wrote Natalie Kalmus in *Coronet* magazine as she described how her dying sister Eleanor, on fire with fever, suddenly rose out of her bed and said: "Natalie. There are so many of them. There's Fred... and Ruth... What's she doing here? Oh, I know!"

Kalmus said an electric shock went through her when she realized that Ruth, their cousin, had suddenly died the week before, but the news had been kept from Eleanor.

As another example of the baffled onlooker, a Dr. Wilson, who witnessed the death of the famous tenor James Moore, told psychical researcher James Hyslop it was "the strangest happening of my life" to see Moore conversing so convincingly in the room allegedly with his deceased, invisible mother, saying, "Just wait, mother, I am almost over. I can jump it. Wait, mother."

Angel-like beings of light are also often reported at the deathbed. An individual who brushed with death but survived the experience told researcher Raymond Moody that he had a vision of a being of light during his crisis.

"He (the being) was telling me that I was going to go on and live this time, but there would be a time when he would be getting in touch with me again, and that I would actually die."

The psychopompic (escorting the dead) being of light may also appear to survivors to herald a coming death:

In *A Book of Angels,* Sophy Burnham reports how country singer Johnny Cash, at age 12, was visited by an angel whose peace-giving radiance filled his room, telling him that his older brother Jack would die. Years later, the angel returned to predict the death of Johnny Horton, Cash's closest friend, helping him to prepare for that passing, too.

Indeed, as St. John Chrysostom, the greatest orator of the early Christian Church, remarked 1,600 years ago: "If we need a guide in passing from one city to another, how much more will the soul need someone to point out the way when she breaks the bonds of the flesh."

Besides take-away apparitions, here are some other things that repeatedly crop up around the time of death:

- The dying often see gorgeous afterworld scenery. The great inventor Thomas Edison, waking out of a coma on his deathbed, whispered to his doctor: "It is very beautiful over there." In Osis and Haraldsson's survey of deathbed visions in India in the early 1970s, there were many descriptions of afterlife scenery: gardens, barriers, snow-capped mountains, a golden light, a lovely room...

- Apparitions of the newly dead may appear miles away from the deathbed to loved ones to announce their passing and say good-bye, as in Scott Degenhardt's case. Parapsychologists refer to this class of encounter as a *crisis apparition*. Crisis apparition cases are important evidence for life after death -- since the witnesses usually have not been told, by normal means, of the loved one's passing. The Degenhardts, for example, were not formally notified of Ron Degenhardt's death until the phone rang, a call that closely followed Scott Degenhardt's vision.

- The dying may find themselves lifted into a transcendental awareness, joy and peacefulness, as often reported by mystics in their raptures. Which brings up a point: A natural death does not seem to be the terrifying, wrenching experience people imagine, to hear the dying tell it: "Dying is the sweetest, tenderest, most sensuous sensation... Death comes disguised as a sympathetic friend. All was serene... It is easy to die. You have to fight to live," wrote former flying ace

Eddie Rickenbacker, referring to his skirting with
death following a plane crash.

Just before their deaths, the dying seem to develop a
mediumistic ability, a foot each in both worlds, with their
attention shifting more and more to the spiritual plane, away
from the physical.

For example, psychical researcher Hyslop cited a
letter written by Dr. Paul Edwards to the British weekly *Light*
in April 1900 in which Edwards reported the comments of a
woman dying of cancer:

"I see people moving -- all in white. The music is
strangely enchanting-- Oh! There is Sadie. She is with me.
And she knows who I am." Her husband blurted out: "Sissy!
You are out of your mind." His wife replied: "Oh, dear! Why
did you call me here again? Now it will be hard for me to go
away again; I was so pleased while there... I am going away
again and will not come back to you even if you call me."

This pendulum of consciousness swinging back and
forth between the two worlds is also illustrated by the deathbed experience of King Paul of Greece in March 1964. Queen
Frederika, who was keeping a vigil, writes:

"I went into the sickroom and found Paul with a
happy look on his face... 'I thought I'd already gone off,' he
said softly. 'I still feel far away. It takes time to get used to
being back...'"

Paul went on to describe a vision he had of a long dark
road with a light shining at the far end -- similar to many
stories told by people brushing with death of how they went
through a dark "tunnel" leading to a world of light. The light
gave the king a sublimely happy and peaceful feeling.

"Yes, now I understand everything," Paul told
Frederika. "This is the most wonderful time of our lives... I
like it very much there... When we get there, everything will
be straightened out... There, we'll be free."

Sometimes, even when there is no life-threatening crisis, the appearance of a departed loved one to fetch someone may signal that that person's death is near -- making the take-away apparition an "angel of death" of sorts.

Osis reported the case of a 70- year-old woman whose deceased husband had appeared to her several times in a window, beckoning to her to come out of her house to join him. As a result, she predicted her death to her family members, laid out her burial clothes, reclined for a nap and died an hour later. The woman's doctor was so surprised at her death that he had her body checked for accidental poisoning, with negative results.

Occasionally, when a take-away apparition appears, the dying vigorously resist. A college-educated Indian man was recovering nicely from mastoiditis, reported Osis and a colleague in India, Erlendur Haraldsson. But at 5 a.m., the Indian man was heard to shout: "Someone is standing here dressed in white clothes. I will not go with you!" He was dead in 10 minutes. So-called "no consent" cases were common in India but rare in America, the researchers noted, perhaps because of cultural differences.

Belief in heavenly beings that come to the deathbed to help in the transition is age-old. The ancient Church fathers assumed that angels come at the moment of death. The ancient Greek philosopher Plato felt guardian spirits do the job.

In the Old Testament, the angel of death is the angel to whom God delegates the power to bring death to mortals. Folklore is full of elaborations. In Jewish lore, the angel of death is covered with eyes so that no mortal can escape his attention. Many Jewish legends have the angel of death showing up at the worst time to claim someone -- a couple's wedding night, for example. A struggle breaks out, and the angel of death is sometimes tricked or cheated or takes pity and agrees to come back another day.

Starting in 1959, psychologist Karlis Osis conducted a famous study of deathbed visions or near-death experiences.

Surveying 35,000 cases, he determined that at least six per cent involved scenic visions or the sighting of apparitions. The numbers of visions may well be much higher, since Osis had to rely for much of his information on doctors and nurses who often are kept in the dark about paranormal phenomena by family members.

The great majority of patients died within 10 minutes of their visions and nearly all of them within a few hours.

Prominent researchers in the field of death-related visions -- from physics professor Sir William Barrett in the 1920s to death-and-dying expert Elizabeth Kuebler-Ross and psychologist Karlis Osis in the 1960s and 1970s -- have independently turned up similar phenomena. Barrett noted that dying children were surprised to see angels without wings.

"It seems that apparitions show a purpose of their own, contradicting the intentions of the patients. This suggests that they are not merely outward projections of the patient's psyche," commented researchers Osis and Haraldsson.

Other circumstantial evidence is that the dying frequently report that someone has come in spirit to their deathbed, when the patient did not know about that person's death. Death-and-dying expert Elizabeth Kuebler-Ross was at the deathbed of a boy who, along with his mother and brother Peter had been in a terrible, fiery auto crash. The mother was killed but Peter survived and was transferred to a burn facility.

When Kuebler-Ross asked Peter's brother how he was doing, the boy said: "Yes, everything is all right now. Mommy and Peter are already waiting for me." Smiling, the boy lapsed into a coma and eventually died. As Kuebler-Ross later learned, Peter had died a short time before his brother.

Ultimately, deathbed visions help us deal with one of the great fears of our culture: that the light goes out at the moment of death. Shakespeare summed it up well, when he had Horatio bid farewell to his fallen friend Hamlet: "Good night, sweet prince, and flights of angels sing thee to thy rest."

9. The Feeling...

One night, a group of cowering teen-agers had only the glass windows of their shelter to protect them from a violent attack by an armed gang trying to force its way inside. Did a mother's prayer miles away make that glass impenetrable?

At that moment, back at the home of two of those boys -- a sense of utter terror came over Janet Frederick[1] -- a gut feeling that her two sons, George and Jerry, were somehow in grave trouble.

Over the years, Janet had learned to trust her subtle intuitive feelings. Once, when her grandparents were in danger of drowning on a vacation thousands of miles away -- Janet had had a premonition of calamity and had prayed for the couple, who were rescued by a passer-by.

Now, the fear for her boys was so intense, it bordered on pain. Janet lay down on her bed, crying. Was it an accident of some sort?

"God, help them. Send your angels to take care of them. Send them home safe to me." She prayed that last sentence over and over.

George and Jerry were trapped -- surrounded by a gang of angry armed youths. The attackers seemed to have come out of nowhere -- rushing up to them from many directions. All around the sanctuary where George and Jerry took shelter they heard the constant thudding of heavy clubs beating hard against windows.

1 Names in this story have been changed

George's eyes were glued to one attacker who stood off at a distance, wielding a firearm, as the others tried to break the glass to get in.

Nearby, a friend of George's crouched down, trembling, when one of the attackers outside mockingly flaunted a gun near one of the windows in the midst of the tumultuous pounding by the clubs.

Elsewhere, another friend of George's and Jerry's was astonished when a solid, heavy club smacked the window right beside his head with full force -- but cracked in pieces. *The club, not the window. The thoroughly ordinary glass window did not suffer the slightest crack!*

In fact, none of the windows was shattering, spidering or even cracking in the least despite the rapid-fire full-force pounding of the heavy wooden clubs for a full minute. A couple of dozen blows or more.

Janet paced the floor. But after about 10 minutes, her panic subsided.

Later, George and Jerry stepped in the door, faces pale.

"Thank God you're home safe!" Janet said.

The story of the attack poured out. And how the gang's assault finally broke off, leaving them unharmed.

Now, George and Jerry could breathe, but they were overwhelmed. What had kept those windows from breaking?! A guy could put his fist through a glass window, a simple rock could break one, to say nothing of crack it. George and Jerry had not been huddled in a steel vault at Fort Knox or an armored Presidential limousine.

After the incident, George thoroughly double-checked the windows where he, Jerry and their friends had taken refuge: There was not the smallest crack in any of the glass.

"Angels or something had to be watching over us," George said.

9. Essay: Premonitions, Hunches, Feelings...

"Sweet souls around us watch us still/ Press nearer to our side/ Into our thoughts, into our prayers/ With gentle helpings glide."
Harriet Beecher Stowe

"Was it an angel who whispered into the ear of one of two drowning shipwreck survivors near England's Goodwin Sands, clinging to a bit of driftwood -- who offered to let go so his companion who had a wife and children would have better odds of surviving?" asked the 19th Century writer Henry Latham.

Where does that inner feeling come from that whispers or shouts to us -- that sudden flash of insight, surge of confidence, sharp twinge of conscience -- that powerful intuition that does not seem to come from ourselves?

Suddenly, we are overwhelmed to do the illogical thing, but it turns out later not only to have been the correct, but only thing we could have done. Even if that thing was simply to pray earnestly for someone's safety when there was no outward sign of trouble.

And is prayer, as a book title once suggested, "the mightiest force on earth?"

On November 29, 1963, businessman Leonard J. Crimp, on his way to Toronto, was preparing to board Air Canada Flight 831 at Montreal International Airport. At the same time, five of Crimp's friends, unbeknownst to each other, began having a feeling that Crimp was in danger and felt impelled to pray for him. The DC-8 took off from the airport. Four minutes later, Flight 831 began losing altitude and crashed amid a ball of fire that mushroomed 100 feet high. All 118 passengers died.

But Crimp himself was safe and unharmed. Just before takeoff, a ground hostess, for some reason never explained, singled Crimp out from those waiting to fly the doomed aircraft and dispatched him to another plane.

William Rauscher, who reported Crimp's case in *The Spiritual Frontier*, asked: "How many fortunate 'coincidences,' I wonder are rooted in somebody's praying? How much of fate is engineered by prayer?"

Was this a case of intervention by benevolent angelic beings who impressed Crimp's friends with the need to pray, as some might argue? Or was it a case of so-called crisis telepathy, where Crimp, on some deep subconscious level unknown to his conscious self, understood his coming predicament and sent out a psychic distress call for help to friends who picked up the signal and responded with prayer? Or perhaps there was some other cause for the "still, small voice" that prodded his friends.

Rauscher quoted psychoanalyst Nandor Fodor: "I believe that the substance of prayer is this: A human anguish spreads all over the universe and may get an answer from the Cosmic Mind."

Whether this intuition that seemingly comes from outside ourselves flashes brilliantly into our minds like lightning or tickles us persistently over time -- it sometimes brings a difficult message to hear -- something we would hate to do but should. Or we may be struck by the striking originality or novelty of the message.

One important telltale sign that an intuition is coming from beyond your limited self: An absolute certainty that something will happen or that something must be done -- no matter how ridiculous it appears.

Our inner whisperings are not just a short-term problem-solving tool -- "freeze at the green light or get hit" -- but also a spur to spiritual growth over the long haul, many argue. A guardian angel works for our "inner unfoldment" and becomes "a compass directing our footsteps," contends theosophical clairvoyant Flower Newhouse. "(The angel's) advice speaks in our intuitions and her teachings in our deepening convictions. She leads us into the long corridor of Overcoming (and when once within that hall of testing, she becomes our examiner and our initiator)."

Creativity itself seems to gush from this source beyond our conscious minds. In fact, our word genius -- a person so inspired by intuition as to have a giant intellect and creativity -- comes from the Latin name of an ancient Roman's inspiring guardian spirit. A Roman woman's inspiring spirit was not a genius but a *juno*.

Poet Emily Dickinson, an artistic genius herself, said in Victorian times that the sudden lighting of the candle of inspiration in your mind may not have been so sudden, after all: "Ah, friend, you little knew/ how long at that celestial wick/ the angels labored diligent."

Scientists sometimes speak of a discovery being "in the air" -- waiting to be "picked up" -- intuited. In the 1600s, for example, calculus "coincidentally" was independently developed, within a span of only a few years, by the English physicist Isaac Newton, and the German philosopher and mathematician Gottfried Wilhelm von Leibnitz.

In the 1800s, the same thing happened. Charles Darwin was ready to publish his theory of evolution when he chanced to receive a manuscript from his naturalist friend Alfred Russel Wallace, based in the East Indies, that set forth the same ideas.

What opens the channels for divine or angelic inspiration to flow? Spiritual purity, for one thing, is often mentioned. "Great artistic works spring from selfless intentions, high aspirations, a passion for beauty and a sense of humbleness that purifies the psyche and allows genius to flow (italics mine)," observes the modern writer Harvey Humann. However, a person's intuitive voice weakens if he becomes impure, corrupt and foolish, the ancient Greek philosopher Plato warned.

Creativity aside -- in general terms, trusting your intuition and acting on it is also said to strengthen this quiet voice. A feedback loop develops. You ask for help. The whisper of advice comes. You follow your inner conviction, despite the difficulty. Strangely, help comes unexpectedly for your courageous effort. Coincidences. People just "popping up" whom you need to meet the challenge. Then, you ask for more advice. With each successful loop, the inner voice intensifies. But ignoring the call of intuition is said to increase the static and lower the reception, so to speak.

Wherever it comes from, the voice of intuition is persuasive but not dictatorial. The whispering angel never tramples our own free will, argued the great medieval theologian Thomas Aquinas, echoing mainstream opinion. We are challenged to *voluntarily* heed, as Lincoln put it, "the better angels of our nature."

How do you tell if your intuitive insights are heavenly inspiration or just your own thinking?

"If the idea ... brings illumination or seems to offer guidance for action in a new direction," comments Theodora Ward, "if it assuages the pain of an inner conflict or gives relief from anxiety caused by outer problems, it may be felt as the direct intervention of a supernatural being."

And if the intuition is from outside yourself, how do you tell if it is divine or angelic, on the one hand, or from a malignant influence, on the other? One yardstick: Does the guidance raise your consciousness, make you more spiritual, move you forward? Or does it increase the darkness, confusion and negativity of your life? This is sometimes cited as a pivotal test for "discerning the spirits," as the New Testament puts it.

Observed Puritan Increase Mather in *Angelographia* in 1696, America's first angel book: "Angels, both good and bad, have a greater influence on this world than men are generally aware of."

10. The Mysterious Stranger...

One night, as Melissa Tidwell was closing up the famous celebrity-frequented Nashville nightclub where she was one of the managers, she noticed that a man who had already been sitting around for hours was still there, plugged into his seat.

"I don't know who you're waiting for. Everybody's gone," Melissa told him.

Chris Deal looked at Melissa and said fondly: "I've been waiting for you."

Chris, a talented session musician and songwriter, and Melissa were eventually married, two happy peas in a pod for seven years.

Then, shortly before Thanksgiving 1980, Chris, normally a high-energy athletic man who ran five miles a day, started un-explainably slowing down. Napping a lot. Ominously, a low-grade fever began. Melissa urged a visit to the doctor.

"Let's wait until after the holidays. It's no big deal," Chris said.

In January, Melissa waited while a G.P. checked Chris over. An hour went by. Two hours. Three. Something terrible was happening. After four and a half hours, Chris emerged with the doctor at his side. Chris' white blood cell count was very high. The suspected diagnosis: leukemia. Melissa sank with the word.

For several months, Chris and Melissa lived on the 11th floor, the leukemia floor, of a cancer hospital in Houston. Chemo pounded the cancer cells -- and the rest of Chris, too. His weight and spirits plunged in tandem. The war was being lost.

Profoundly depressed, Chris was a hollow shell of his one-time vibrant self -- sleeping most of the day. He had to be helped as his thin frame shuffled to the bathroom, dragging two I.V. poles along.

At night, any slight grunt or cough from Chris' bed, and Melissa's eyes popped open. But one night, the hair-trigger sleeper slept unusually deeply. Then: *Wake up!* As her eyes opened, a frantic-faced nurse was shaking her. It was 3 a.m. Chris' bed was empty.

"We cannot find Chris," the nurse said.

In a panic, Melissa shot out into the hallway. She passed the nurses station, which was an all-seeing island in the center of a circular ward. It was manned continually, and every patient leaving his room would have to go past it -- including someone as conspicuous as Chris with the two I.V. poles in tow. They had seen nothing.

Out of the corner of an eye, Melissa glimpsed movement inside the eleventh floor's petite generic chapel. She looked in. *There was Chris!* Melissa threw the door open. "Chris! Where have you been? I was so afraid!"

Chris was sitting on a plastic chair directly across from a strange-looking young man -- so close their knees almost touched. They were talking.

"It's okay, Melissa. Go back to the room. Everything's okay," Chris said.

"Chris, what's going on? Where have you been? Everybody's upset."

"Please -- go back to the room. Everything's okay."

Unnerved, Melissa looked more closely at the slight, smallish stranger. Was he dangerous? What was he doing here at 3 a.m.?

The stranger was quiet, his eyes on the floor, as if to avoid attention. A teen-age youth. Perfectly formed, extremely pale skin. White-blond hair, cut short. Oddly, the youth looked like he had just walked out of a clothing store, wearing his new purchases. The flannel shirt, the stiff jeans and lace-up work boots seemed just minutes off the shelf.

Still, despite its newness, it was just the sort of casual clothing that a session musician like Chris might wear himself.

Suddenly, the stranger looked up at Melissa dead-on with icy blue eyes -- colored more like a Husky dog's than a human's. There was a startling brightness about those eyes. Melissa sensed a peacefulness -- and a wisdom about him that contradicted his young age.

"O.K.," Melissa said, still reluctant.

A wave of relief swept over the nurse's station when Melissa stopped by there on her way back to the room.

A half-hour later, Chris was at the door of the room with an ear-to-ear grin on his face and his two constant companions, the I.V. poles, at his side. Sure, it looked like Chris, but could it really be him? This patient who hours earlier could only be roused from slumber with difficulty was now full of energy, excited. This was the man she had met years ago and had gradually lost.

"Who was that guy?" Melissa asked. Chris' dimples imploded on his cheeks as the grin returned.

"You're never going to believe me... He was an angel... my guardian angel."

But Melissa did. Right away, she did. Something extraordinary had happened to this man.

Now, Melissa was back into the hallway for her second run that night. First stop: the chapel. Nobody there. Down the elevator she went to the main hospital lobby. A security guard posted there said he saw no pale flaxen-haired sapphire-eyed youth with clothes that should have had their price stickers still attached.

"No one's seen him," Melissa said as she returned to Chris, who sat on his bed, still smiling.

"Maybe he got off on another floor," she added.

Chris burst out laughing. "Okay, Melissa, if that makes you feel better, you can believe that," Chris commented.

"What happened?" Melissa asked. Her questions flew thick and fast.

Chris told her he had been "jerked awake" near 3 a.m. As he opened his eyes, he had an overwhelming feeling that he should go to the floor's chapel.

"I was summoned," Chris told Melissa. "You were put to sleep."

When he entered the chapel, Chris dropped to his knees and started praying. Suddenly, a voice behind him asked: "Are you Chris Deal?" Chris turned around. The young tow-headed man was standing there. They started talking.

"Is there anything you want to be forgiven for?" the stranger asked. Chris said there was a relative he had always hated. He wanted the hate to go away and to be forgiven for that.

"Well, you have been forgiven," the visitor said.

"I'm worried about Melissa."

"She'll be fine. Don't worry." Then: "Would you like to say the rosary."

Chris had not mentioned he was Catholic. But they did say the rosary together. The conversation explored various other areas of Chris' life, and finally the stranger said:

"Chris, all your prayers have been answered."

For the next three days, the old Chris was back in force, laughing heartily, enjoying food he previously would hardly touch, joking and talking with Melissa as they stayed up late to watch TV. He even went from room to room on his ward, inspiring patients with his reinvigorated presence. He shed one of his I.V. poles -- the one with the vitamins. The doctors were very en couraged.

But on the morning of the third day -- the first anniversary of the day he was diagnosed -- the spell was suddenly broken.

That morning, Melissa woke up and noticed Chris lying on his side and staring at her.

"What?" Melissa asked.

"I dreamed about Bill last night," Chris said. "It was real vague. But I told you I'd tell you." There was concern in Chris' tone for Melissa's feelings, but no fear.

Tears came to Melissa's eyes. Bill was a fellow song-writer and a best friend of Chris'. He had been killed in a car wreck, and Melissa had always had the feeling that if Chris had ever had a vision of him, Chris' time would be near. Bill would be coming for him to help him in the transition, the great crossing.

At 4 p.m. that afternoon -- on the anniversary of his diagnosis, almost to the hour -- Chris suddenly collapsed as he and Melissa sat side by side. Melissa moved to help him. But he was dead in minutes -- of a burst heart artery.

"I do believe that a miracle did take place. His physical body didn't survive, but his spiritual body was healed," Melissa says. Whatever grand journey Chris was now embarked upon, he went out whole, strong and prepared for it.

"I believe that our material bodies are just space suits for the earth experience. (The body) gets damaged and hurt and finally doesn't work for us anymore, and we leave it. But what's inside, the undying spiritual self is the real us," Melissa says.

Each person comes to earth on a mission, she adds, and Chris' foreshortened life taught her about the things that make life, whatever its length, worth living -- faith and spirituality.

10. Essay: The Angel in Disguise...

"Remember to welcome strangers in your home. There were some who did that and welcomed angels without knowing it."
Letter to the Hebrews

"An angel! Or if not, an earthly paragon!"
William Shakespeare

The angel in disguise. He looks just like a human being and helps you out in the most ordinary way -- fixing a flat, directing you in a confusing airport... But he helps you amid so many uncanny, bizarre circumstances, that by the time the incident is all over, you're shaking your head and wondering... Could that really have been a human being?

It's not a blazing being of light or a thundering supernatural voice, nor even a screaming feeling in your gut. This category of en counter is far more subtle, vague -- custom-designed by heaven to send the die-hard skeptic into a howling fit.

What, typically, are the bizarre circumstances that tend to crop up again and again in this genre of angel encounter?

- A seemingly human helper appears out of nowhere when the crisis begins. After solving the problem, the helper vanishes again just as suddenly. Even though there was no place he could have quickly come from or departed to.

- The stranger's face often has a compelling, attractive or noble-featured look. The eyes are particularly noticeable -- bright and expressive.

- The helper knows things about the person being assisted that he should not know. Yet he avoids answering questions about himself, and if he does, the information doesn't check out later.

• If an article or object is needed, he "happens" to show up with it.

• The helper not only solves the immediate physical problem, if there is one, but also delves into the psychological problem: "Don't worry. That new boss of yours who is giving everyone such a hard time won't last. You're thinking of quitting, but just hang on. He'll be out the door in another two weeks." How did he know about that?

To top it off, the person being helped often does not notice how strange everything is until the helper is gone:

"Very often the recognition comes only in retrospect," wrote Nancy Gibbs in a Time Magazine cover story on angels. "A person is in immediate danger -- the car stalled in the deadly snowstorm, the small plane lost in the fog, the swimmer too far from shore. And emerging from the moment's desperation comes some logical form of rescue: a tow truck driver, a voice from the radio tower, a lifeguard. But when the victim is safe and turns to give thanks, the rescuer is gone. There are no tire tracks in the snow. There is no controller in the tower. and there are no footprints on the beach."

Dutch physician Hans Moolenburgh, whose angel investigations made headlines in Europe, illustrates this "recognition in retrospect" with the story of a couple trapped in a raging mountain snowstorm who contacted him about their experience. In *Meetings With Angels*, Moolenburgh notes that the couple was driving through a gale-force snowstorm in the Pyrenees mountains of Andorra along a steep, deadly ravine, buffeted by 84 mile- per-hour wind gusts. When the roads became extremely slick, the car slid to the very edge of the ravine, making it impossible to back away. Yet the car was now a sitting duck in the poor visibility to be struck by another vehicle. The driver had no idea how to put on snow chains, although he had them.

Suddenly, a neatly dressed, friendly man walked up in the middle of the blinding snowstorm, pushed the car away from the ravine, took the snow chains out of the car's boot and put them on. Then, having said nothing to the couple, the man started to walk away.

The driver followed him, offering profuse thanks. The man walked off in the opposite direction from which he had come -- so he had obviously not come from a parked car.

Only then -- after the stranger was gone -- did the couple realize something extremely strange: Although the man had walked to and from their car in a raging snowstorm and had fitted snow tires, *he had walked off without a snow-flake on him.*

"Contact with heaven," comments Moolenburgh, "often produces a dream-like change of consciousness, so that something which might have seemed bizarre or strange at another time, now seems normal, or goes unnoticed. In our dreams, we do not think it strange that we can fly, although we know that this is impossible when we are awake."

It happens that one of TV's most famous angels -- Jonathan Smith, on the long-running show *Highway to Heaven* -- is an angel in disguise, the very soul of discretion. Smith looks quite human, even dresses casually. Just as in the encounters in real life, Smith's actions on the surface seem so natural, so non-magical to the humans he deals with.

"He wouldn't use supernatural powers to solve prob-lems; he would persuade human beings to solve them by helping one another," wrote the late actor Michael Landon -- who played Smith -- in the December 1986 Guideposts article, *A Bit of Heaven on Earth.*

In 1990, Jocelyn Veile and her friend Laura were hiking on a high, desolate, rubble-strewn mountain in the country of Uruguay in South America. When they lost their path, and their progress upward was virtually halted by an unbroken carpet of jagged boulders, they cried and prayed.

Jocelyn and Laura decided to inch their way back down the soaring mountain. Shouting and screaming, they got colder and colder as darkness closed in.

Then, in the mid-winter twilight, a Spanish-speaking man with friendly eyes and a weather-beaten face appeared out of nowhere, high on the deserted mountain, and stopped the two teen-age girls -- just before they were about to unknowingly plunge off a deadly cliff. He took their hands to lead them. Soon afterward, he lifted the girls past another dangerous drop-off and then led them down to the foot of the mountain.

At the bottom, there was a lot of hugging and crying when Jocelyn's teary red-faced mother, Jeannette, came up. The stranger told Jocelyn's translator that the girls were 10 feet from the cliff when he stopped them.

The girls, Jeannette, the translator, and the stranger now walked together as a group on gravely ground. But suddenly, the stranger was not with them. Jocelyn and Laura looked backward and saw something odd -- to add to the growing list of oddities. It was only hours later that the two girls worked up the nerve to tell one another what each had independently noticed at that moment: Three sets of tracks were unbroken. *But the stranger's tracks suddenly stopped -- and went nowhere.*

"I was going through a low spot in my spiritual life," Jocelyn said. "A lot of my friends at school were trying to convince me that God didn't exist or didn't care. When I came back, I was able to say, 'Look, you're wrong. God isn't a fictional character or... optional.'"

In medieval times, people were familiar with the angel-in-disguise phenomenon. Philosophers quibbled about this issue in their airy debates of logic. (Such debates over the finer points of angels were called *quodlibets*.) One of the quodlibets was: "If an angel comes to earth and takes on a physical human body for its mission, what happens to that body when the angel goes back to heaven?"

Incidentally, the most famous quodlibet -- "How many angels can dance on the head of a pin?" -- was supposedly not ever really debated by medieval philosophers but made up by modern types to ridicule these medieval debates.

(The answer, by the way, is that all of the angels in the universe can stand on the tiniest speck of a pinpoint with all the space left over because, as some philosophers believed, angels have no mass or matter, therefore take up no space.)

Indeed, angels do seem to sometimes move among us incognito -- as the powerful Russian Czar Peter the Great disguised himself 300 years ago to mix with the ordinary people of Europe.

11. The Animal...

When his master was struggling to survive in the wreckage of a car that tumbled off a cliff, did the dog's love for him cause it to come back from the dead to summon help?

In 1982, Shawn, a Seattle paramedic, and his partner were called to the area of a terrible accident that had occurred in rainy weather. But the ambulance, arriving at the unlit, isolated scene around midnight could not locate the exact spot.

Then, Shawn dimly noticed something coming up over the edge of a cliff toward the rolling ambulance. Shawn's partner stopped the unit and shone a bright light in the direction of the moving object. It was a dog -- a distinctive, yellow golden retriever. *Very odd.*

"He started to bark and pulled me along," Shawn recalled. "I grabbed my light and shined it down (the cliff) and didn't see anything. He kept turning around and insisting that I follow him down into the brush."

Shawn returned to the ambulance, fetched a portable light and then let the dog lead him down the cliff.

At last, Shawn saw a vehicle's taillight reflecting in the glare of his light. Here was the wreck! Shawn radioed for help, then moved inside the car to the front seat, finding the seriously injured motorist badly pinned inside.

The vehicle had rolled over several times on the road above before plunging down the embankment.

The victim was finally extricated from the twisted mass of metal, strapped to a backboard, and loaded on the ambulance. Somehow, in all the excitement, the mysterious Golden Retriever had disappeared.

An hour or two later, once Shawn and his partner were back at their station, another call came in, telling them to return to the scene of the accident. *What for? Had they accidentally left some equipment there?*

When Shawn arrived, he saw emergency personnel at the scene. The utterly smashed car had been pulled up the cliff.

"It was just totally crushed. It was hard to believe anybody could have lived through it," Shawn said.

A firefighter struck up a conversation, and Shawn mentioned that "we just found this one guy."

"No," the firefighter responded. "Didn't you look in the back seat?"

Shawn looked the back of the car. *Sprawled on the back seat was a dead Golden Retriever. It had been crushed and killed instantly.* Shawn's hair stood up on the back of his neck. He turned to his partner: "Didn't you see that dog?"

"No, what dog?"

Shawn recalled for his partner how he had seen a golden retriever just like the one in the wreckage come up over the top of the cliff and lead him down into the brush where the wrecked vehicle was.

"No, I never saw a dog," his partner reiterated.

11. Essay: Spiritual Intervention by Animals...

"Heaven goes by favor. If it went by merit, you would stay out and your dog would go in."
Mark Twain

Stories like this one, which I heard from Shawn while I was a guest on the Laura Lee talk show in Seattle, remind us why "Fido" has been a traditional name for our loving dogs. It means "I am faithful" in Latin.

A common category of spiritual intervention involves animals interacting with humans -- rescuing, guarding or just nurturing. Often a pet with a master.

Sometimes the person who is helped feels that the animal itself in spirit form has returned to the physical world.

In a first-person article in *Fate* Magazine, Ronald Adkins discussed his beloved dog Pat, who had died from the strain of tropical heat after master and pet moved to the Caribbean from England.

Following Pat's death, Adkins was out strolling when he was confronted by muggers demanding money. Somehow, it was Pat who burst out of bushes, terrifying the would-be robbers and chasing them away.

"I shall never forget the look of intense love Pat gave me just before he disappeared. That was my introduction to the supernatural," Adkins said.

In a slightly different type of experience -- it is a living animal moving in to help -- either acting on its own will or inspired by some higher power. In Old Testament legend, for example, the out-of-favor prophet Elijah flees to the desert to hide. There, he is cared for by ravens who bring him food at God's command.

Modern parallels to this story abound. During World War II, flying ace Eddie Rickenbacker went missing after being shot down over the Pacific. Mayor Fiorello LaGuardia asked all New York City to pray for him. After his rescue, Rickenbacker revealed that a gull had appeared from nowhere, perching on his head -- which he grabbed and killed for food for himself and fellow survivors.

"I have no explanation except that God sent one of his angels to rescue us," Rickenbacker said.

In the late 1970s, the popular *People's Almanac II* reported how a giant sea turtle saved the life of 52-year-old Candelaria Villanueva.

Villaneuva was left floating for 48 hours in the Pacific Ocean with only a life jacket after her ship, the *Aloha,* caught fire and sank 600 miles south of Manila. Villaneuva said she had been in the water for half a day when the turtle, "with a head as big as that of a dog," appeared under her.

On June 4, the Philippine navy ship *Kalantia* caught sight of Villaneuva. The crew pitched her a life preserver, thinking that she was holding on to an oil drum.

"The moment she transferred her hold to the ring, the drum sank. We did not realize it was a giant turtle until we started hauling up the woman, for the turtle was beneath her, apparently propping her up," a crew member was quoted as saying.

Other familiar living animal-saves-man stories include dolphins beaching drowning sailors or animals popping up out of nowhere to ward off a threat to someone -- for example, a powerful stray dog showing up suddenly to escort a nervous woman walking home, being subtly followed by a seedy-looking man.

In these cases, is the living animal guided by angels to help, has an angel just taken the form of an animal, or is there some other explanation?

In another major series of spiritual stories involving animals, an animal's sudden appearance may symbolize something in the life of the person witnessing it. Or the appearance may foreshadow a change to come.

One of the most common animal-as-symbol themes is death. Carl Jung, one of the giants of psychiatry in the 20th Century, had a female patient who noticed a pattern: birds collected outside the window of the rooms where her mother and, on another occasion, her grandmother were dying.

Later, the woman became anxious when an entire flock of birds swarmed her house shortly after her husband had been sent by Jung to a doctor for a medical check-up. Although the physician found nothing wrong, the man was mortally stricken after leaving the office and brought home dying.

12. The Fragrance...

Did a Mississippi River barge hand continue to show his love for an ailing niece he befriended as a child -- saying it with flowers from beyond the grave?

In her early thirties, Terry Booker began developing lupus, a painful auto-immune disease. It was then that strange things began happening around her house in the small Mississippi town where she grew up.

On "bad days" of pain or depression, Terry's house would often become filled with the strong fragrance of magnolia blossoms, although there were no trees in her yard or even on the road where she lived. Visitors entering the house commented on the smell of a potpourri mixture, when in fact there was no potpourri set out.

On one occasion, Terry was up all night, tormented by pain in her bones and joints. Husband Carl tried in vain to get her to go to the hospital. Finally, that morning, Terry dozed off.

Suddenly, after only a moment or two, she was awake again -- feeling the weight of someone sitting on the bed behind her. She stretched out her arm behind her to touch Carl but felt only empty space. Turning over, she saw no one there. At the same instant, though, she suddenly noticed the scent of magnolia again. This time, the smell was so overpowering that it almost nauseated her.

Soon, Carl returned to the house from a quick visit to his office and, before Terry could mention it, he remarked that the house had a floral smell.

"Can this really be happening, or am I crazy?" Terry thought, as she lay on the bed, musing. Terry hatched the idea to place ads in three women's magazines to see if any other people had had this kind of experience with scents.

Carl suggested signing the ad with a pseudonym to protect their privacy. So Terry sat down to think one up. She spontaneously wrote down "Curtis" -- her mother's maiden name. That would be the surname.

Now, all she needed were some initials to go with it. She began writing down letter combinations at random. But two letters: *C.J.* kept coming to her mind over and over.

"It wrote so easy, and it felt right," Terry recalls.

One day, Terry and her mother went to the post office to check the response to the ads. There was a big stack of mail waiting.

Her mother's eyes fell on the envelopes, all addressed to the pseudonym *"C.J. Curtis."*

"You know, C.J. Curtis is the name of your Uncle Clarence," she mentioned to Terry. *Snap!* The strange pieces of Terry's seven-year puzzle -- the recurring magnolia smell, that presence in her room behind her after her difficult night of pain -- suddenly it all came together.

Could it really be Clarence?! Her thoughts went back to her childhood...

Clarence Jefferson Curtis, her uncle, had had no family of his own, and Terry's family had become surrogates. Clarence took a particular liking to Terry, a sickly child suffering from a bone inflammation disease.

Doctors even decided at one point to amputate Terry's leg, but her tears and shouts of protest moved the grown-ups to try instead the painful ordeal of antibiotic injections into the knee cap and leg bone. Terry could not walk as a result.

The thirtyish Clarence, when not plying the Mississippi as a hand on a barge, often visited Terry's house -- frequently bringing a hand-picked bouquet of magnolia blossoms to present to Terry, along with presents. Grandma would fuss some about the mess the blossoms made after they opened up, but Clarence knew the little girl loved flowers.

Terry's leg was saved, and she went on to a career as a registered nurse.

After the post office visit with her mother, Terry knew what to say when friends entered her house, asking: "What is that? It smells so good." She answers forthrightly that it is her deceased uncle.

Today, Terry's lupus is in remission, and the magnolia scent no longer comes as often to her or her visitors, but at times she still senses the presence of her caring uncle.

Essay: Fragrances Signaling the Presence of the Heavenly Side

Most contact stories involving the senses usually amount to seeing an apparition, hearing a voice, or feeling an invisible "force." The sense of smell crops up less often, but there is also a long history behind olfactory experiences -- ranging from saints to mediums.

In his *Encyclopedia of Psychic Science,* psychoanalyst and psychic researcher Nandor Fodor discusses the "perfumes" or fragrances which sometimes crop up during seances, either allegedly produced by the mediums themselves or by spirits entering the room.

Fodor also notes that, considering this phenomenon, the Church's religious expression "the odor of sanctity" should be looked at in a new light. He cites, for example, legends of saints in which their bodies were said to emit pleasant scents ranging from orange blossom (St. Cajetan) to musk (St. Francis).

Most reports, however, seem simply to occur spontaneously among regular people. As in Terry's story above and the following account, the scent often carries meaning:

In December 1972, after an Eastern Airlines jumbo jet crashed in the Florida Everglades, one of the fatalities, Second Officer Don Repo, allegedly started making his presence felt to his widow Alice, according to author John G. Fuller, who interviewed her.

One night, for example, an overpowering odor of Vitalis in her bedroom woke Alice up. The smell of Vitalis -- which Don had frequently used in life -- was coming from a pillow next to her. But no Vitalis had been in the Repo home for the past year, and the pillows were clean and new. In fact, the fragrance did not disappear from the room until well into the next day.

On a different night, Alice awoke to feel the presence of Don next to her in bed. She reached out in the darkness and felt a hand, then carefully felt of the ring finger. His wedding ring was there -- even a characteristic dent in the ring that she recalled. A feeling of peace and love came over her.

The entire account appears in Fuller's *The Ghost of Flight 451.*

Renee E. Mastalli, in a letter to author Sophy Burnham published in *Angel Letters,* describes how she sat in her home "lost and lonely," unable to stop crying, about a year after her husband died. All of a sudden, an overpowering fragrance of flowers filled the living room where she sat. At that moment, the phone rang -- a friend calling for permission to visit.

When friend Millie entered the house shortly afterward, she remarked about the smell of flowers. Renee realized that Millie also smelled them. Millie asked Renee what her husband's favorite flower was, and when Renee answered, gardenias, Millie theorized that Till was present in the house, telling Renee not to cry over him.

With that remark, the scent of flowers suddenly went away.

The other side of the coin with fragrance phenomena is unpleasant odors, also allegedly manifested by spirits, particularly in hauntings.

13. The Chorus...

After Agnes Rippen[1] found the parking ticket, she knew it was true: Her husband, Dennis, was hooked on tranquillizers.

The ticket was for parking in a fire lane in front of the drug store, and the pharmacist confirmed he had been taking valium. Lots of it, it turned out.

What started out at five to 15 milligrams a day to handle a stressful job had ballooned to 100 milligrams daily.

Dennis did his best to hide it. But he couldn't hide how he had changed from a cheerful, loving husband into a sullen, withdrawn and foggy-minded man, falling asleep at odd moments, even at the wheel.

For several days, Agnes quietly built her case, including exhibit A, the ticket. Then, one Sunday night in the kitchen came the grand confrontation. Agnes methodically presented the state's evidence, item by item, to Dennis.

How do you explain this? This? This?

He's lying to me! she thought as he denied it all with faltering logic -- the first time she had ever known him to be untruthful with her. *Something's taking my husband away from me, and I'm going to fight it!*

Agnes herself had broken the chains of alcoholism and drug addiction eight years earlier. She knew there was only one way out: "You have to admit the problem and get help -- or leave," she told him.

The denials -- the thrust and parry -- continued. The words of Jesus came to Agnes' mind: *"I am the way, the truth*

1. Names in this story have been changed

and the life." She kept repeating it to herself mentally to stay calm -- her life and the life of her loved one were at stake.

Neither harsh accusations nor pleading would turn him. *Stay firm. Don't get scared. And don't dissolve into a teary emotional mush.*

Gradually, Agnes became aware of a great "spiritual pressure" in the kitchen -- like the weight of one's conscience bearing down -- but literally making the air feel heavy and dense. Supporting her -- and urging Dennis.

Agnes set midnight as the deadline. It came without resolution, and she went to bed, her life in ruins. Dennis would be gone tomorrow, and she would have to put on her customary happy face for dozens of people at the office.

As her head hit the pillow -- a mental voice from outside herself, dark and mocking, spoke in her mind: "See. Everything you believe is a lie. Prayer didn't work. And God has failed you."

Agnes sat bolt upright. "*No!* That's not true! Jesus is the way, the truth and the life!" Silence.

Seconds later, the bedroom door opened. Dennis walked to the foot of the bed. "It's all true. I really do need help."

Agnes and Dennis were a knot of arms in the bed, hugging and crying. "I know the worst of the battle is over now, and tomorrow we'll get some help," Agnes said through the tears.

Dennis, freighted with valium, fell quickly asleep. But Agnes' mind was racing.

Jubilant, bursting with gratitude, she walked back to the kitchen battlefield and dropped to her knees, screwed her eyes shut, thanking God out loud and repeatedly.

Suddenly, a swirl of unearthly beautiful music surrounded her. It was a gigantic chorus of awe-inspiring voices and musical instruments from trumpets to strings.

Tinkly, pinging and full-bodied sounds grew into melodies that had hundreds of harmonies.

Agnes opened her eyes. The kitchen's stucco ceiling had disappeared, opening out into a limitless cosmic expanse. Singing, white-robed angels floated around in a misty, three-dimensional Sistine Chapel religious scene.

She was transfixed for a few long minutes, then the image faded and mundane reality crowded back in.

So this was the "spiritual pressure" she had sensed earlier in this kitchen. Was this how the shepherds of the Gospel of Luke felt when a chorus of angels suddenly appeared to them outside Bethlehem?

"Afterwards, I realized that there truly had been a spiritual battle going on in the next dimension, right there in that room. I believe that both sides of that battle presented themselves to me during that experience," Agnes recalled.

The next day, when Dennis got home from work, Agnes and some of their friends, who were familiar with drug treatment, had Dennis' bags packed and waiting for him -- not for a legal separation but a trip to the detox center.

Since 1987, Dennis has been drug-free and still follows the 12-step program.

13. Angelic Music...

"What know we of the Blest above, but that they sing, and that they love?"
William Wordsworth

"This is my Father's world/ And to my listening ears/ All nature sings, and round me rings/ The music of the spheres"
Maltbie D. Babcock

"The angels all were singing out of tune/ And hoarse from having little else to do/ Excepting to wind up the sun and moon/ Or curb a runaway young star or two."
Lord Byron

Is human music just the palest echo of a heavenly music so sublime that, as one experiencer once told parapsychologist D. Scott Rogo, she would gladly die to get a chance to hear it a second time?

This rapturous music is sometimes reported heard by the dying, by those on out-of-body flights, saints deep in prayer, or ordinary folk in a sudden, unplanned moment of great sensitivity.

"The greatest music on earth, be it Brahms or Bach, is nothing but an inharmonious jangle of crude sounds by comparison... It seemed to be produced by vast numbers... incredibly beautiful, clearly superhuman..." said psychical researcher Raymond Bayless of his own experience, quoted by his acquaintance, Rogo, in a magazine article, *The Harmonies of Heaven.*

After receiving the stigmata in his last years -- the marks of Christ's crucifixion -- on his body, the now-blind St. Francis of Assisi had various ecstasies and heavenly flights, during which he had visions of the afterlife and heard celestial music, according to medieval Church legends. As far back as 2,500 years ago, the Greek philosopher Pythagoras spoke of "the music of the spheres."

Today, some modern yoga schools argue that a "life stream in the universe" makes heavenly sounds that a meditator can sometimes hear, Rogo noted. Those fortunate enough to experience the music, called *Nad* by the yogis, sometimes report hearing vast numbers of musical units in exquisite harmony. The music often is first perceived as faint, and in the distance. The listener becomes entranced, overwhelmed. Eventually, the music typically fades out.

Artists doing their best to show this intangible celestial music on canvas put harps in the hands of angels as symbols of Nad -- or equip angels with various other musical instruments, as in many of the great Renaissance angel paintings.

In 1689, the *Letters of Pastor Jurieu* talked about dozens of cases of supernatural music being heard during a widespread religious persecution in France. The music ranged from invisible choirs and ghostly trumpets to psalm singing. In Orthez, where a church was destroyed, a majority of townfolk claimed to hear supernatural music. Authorities in two regions levied fines of up to 5,000 crowns against pilgrims traveling to hear such music.

Sometimes, the music may be accompanied by seeing beautiful heavenly vistas of different types -- including a "Sistine Chapel" scene reminiscent of the sweeping heavenly paintings by the Italian renaissance artist Michelangelo on the ceiling of the famous Vatican chapel bearing the name of Pope Sixtus IV.

In 1742, at the time London composer George Handel wrote the in spiring score of *The Messiah* including its stirring *Hallelujah Chorus*, he said of a grand vision he had had: "I did think I did see all heaven before me and the Great God Himself."

Carol Ann Durepos, a New Mexico graphoanalyst coping with family difficulties and the death of a friend, was praying at an evening mass when suddenly the entire sanctuary seemed to be filled up with colorful "moving light, flashes and singing."

"I felt like the angels, saints, seraphim and cherubim were all rejoicing with me and that the very universe, even the stones, sings praise when the name of Jesus is said or spoken," Durepos told writer Rosemary Guiley, author of *Angels of Mercy.*

The church seemed ready to burst open with the activity, according to Durepos, and she said the name of Jesus felt to her like "a caress to the Father..."

14. The Gentle Touch...

Ten-year-old Paul Swope was so excited as he ran into his house, waving a report card with good grades. But quickly, the youngster sensed that something was wrong. It was something no child should have to face.

Sister Hazel, the 16-year-old first-born, stood at the door to the parents' bedroom with a frightened look on her face. Grandmother had tears in her eyes. Four-year-old kid sister Babe was in her playpen crying.

Paul thought: What hasn't Mother scooped up Babe to comfort her like she always does? Paul rushed to the bedroom.

A doctor stood over Mother, who lay very still. The M.D. took his stethoscope away from the body and shook his head. Paul's father, sitting in a corner, moaned and ran his hands through his hair. Hazel started screaming. Babe was still crying.

Paul's grandmother took his hand and led him gently from the room for a talk. Paul's mother had had pains in her stomach and had been weak for several days. Now, she was going to God.

No, I don't believe it!

But reality sank in when they took Emma Swope's body away. Paul's father, Richard, had paid scant attention to him over the years, and Paul found himself looking up at the sky and praying that his mother -- who was so close to him -- would come back and that it wasn't really true.

In a deep depression, the boy rocked in his mother's rocking chair, trying to recall verbatim all the after-supper stories and songs she had read or sung to him and Babe from that rocker -- when Babe nestled in her lap and Paul sat on the floor, his back against Emma's lower legs and knees. As Babe had gotten older and more clever, she had started teasingly dropping her hand to tug with curled fingers on Paul's hair. Emma's story-telling did not miss a beat as the mother loosened Babe's grip, swept Paul's hair back in place and tenderly stroked her son's forehead. The gentle patting sometimes interrupted Paul's daydreams of being the hero of his mother's pioneer and cowboy stories -- his favorite kind of tale.

But imagining the happy times didn't help the pain, as he had hoped. After the funeral, at bedtime, Paul stared at his ceiling, sobbing, night after night. He was so terribly alone. Dad never seemed to be home any longer. Grandmother did move in at the Ashland, N.J. house. But preschooler Babe, not old enough to under stand the tragedy and quickly forgetting her mother, followed and hugged Grandmother. The lion's share of Grandmother's attention was focused on the smaller Babe.

Please, Mother, come back.

Then, one night, while he cried in bed, Paul suddenly felt a cool hand stroking his forehead and straightening his hair -- as if Babe had tangled and tugged it again and... *Mother!* Paul's hand snapped up to his forehead to grab that hand from heaven and not let it go. For a fleeting second, he felt warm and soft fingers and a powerful love that penetrated him deeply. And peacefulness.

The pain of loss continued long after that night. But Paul now knew he had not been deserted. His mother was nearby, watching over him from his New Jersey childhood, to his adolescence as a flyweight boxer, through a battlefield hell in France during World War II to the raising of a family of his own.

"Even as he was lying here at home and knew he was dying, he would say that wherever she was, she could see him and cared," his widow Alice Swope said. "It was his belief that she cared that kept him going through the crises in his life."

Paul Swope, an Oregon house painter known for his kindness, died in June 1990 at age 74.

14. Essay: The Heavenly Caress...

A World War I colonel whose regiment had been wiped out had an extraordinary experience as he walked up and down a trench. He could feel his soldiers' hands and sense their presence.

"I tell you," he said to songwriter Geoffrey O'Hara, "there is no death." Inspired, O'Hara used those last four words as the title of one of his greatest songs, and the composer later discussed the incident with his friend, positive thinking author Norman Vincent Peale.

"Eternity does not start with death," Peale commented. "We are in eternity now."

Incidents involving touch may also take the form of a characteristic gesture by a departed loved one or in some other way identify the loved one trying to make contact -- as in the Swope story.

Too, the touch may be interpreted as being that of an angel or God Himself. And the purpose may not be merely to comfort or contact the bereaved but to heal or sustain.

Sarah Peebles of Tennessee believes divine intervention was responsible for breaking a two-week fever that had threatened the life of her infant son decades ago. One night, as she dozed off, holding the child in her arms in a rocking chair, she was suddenly awakened by a warm hand on her shoulder. When she opened her eyes, she still felt the warmth on her shoulder, but could see no one. Sarah checked her baby. He was alert and the dangerous fever had finally broken.

Harold B. Lee, the 11th president of the Mormon Church, told the Salt Lake Tabernacle congregation how an invisible blessing hand touched his head twice during a cross-country flight. Soon after he landed, he suffered a massive hemorrhage that would have been fatal had it occurred on the flight, when the "healing hand" touched his head.

15. The Seen and Unseen Helper...Three Vignettes...

- A precocious three-year-old once asked me after a Christmas church function why Charles (pseudonym) was "like Jesus" and had come back from the dead. After I did some open-ended questioning, it turned out the child was claiming to have seen a grieving widow's recently deceased husband, Charles, standing at her side, smiling and patting her shoulder, as she was reading to the children the story of the angels and the shepherds from the Gospel of Luke during the church function. Midway through the widow's reading, the husband's apparition took his hand from her shoulder and strode out of the Sunday School building, with the child's curious eyes following, the child reported. The husband, strangely, was dressed completely in black, including a black cap and shoes, perhaps symbolizing death. And he had on his favorite leather jacket, which the three-year-old knew nothing about but described accurately.

- When baby Allison stopped breathing because of croup -- mother Carole Moore (pseudonym), ran outside her apartment, screaming for help. Nobody responded. Then, something intangible seemed to take over. Tranquillity came. *A sudden thought: She once took a safety course.* Carole visualized the resuscitation. Allison was revived. Later, daughter Julie, almost 3, repeatedly asked Carole about the man Julie saw beside Carole. His hand was on Carole's shoulder during the crisis, Julie said. But Carole saw nobody. Carole's complete story appears in a roundup article on several angel encounters, *I Met an Angel,* in the December 1992 *Ladies' Home Journal.*

- A second croup story: Justine and her husband were in for a shock when they returned home from an evening out. Their baby sitter told them that an ambulance was rushing to the hospital with their baby daughter, who had stopped breathing after a severe attack of croup. In fact, the baby sitter had discovered the child turning blue only because she had heard ''voices'' in the baby's room and had entered the chamber to check things out. But she found no one inside, just the baby -- alone, unbreathing and unconscious. Ten days after the child's life was saved -- the baby's older sister, two years and two months old, spontaneously started talking about angels, without any prompting in a family that Justine said had not been particularly religious and had never discussed angels. The two year old said that an angel had ridden with her as she accompanied her sister in the ambulance to the hospital. There were ''people she didn't know in the ambulance'' and ''they stayed with her in the hospital.'' Explained Justine: ''We tried to get her to be clear about it. She would point up and say it was a man. She described it very clearly, over and over again and was so filled with energy when she was describing it that you almost couldn't get her to sit down.'' Justine says she now very strongly believes in angels. Justine shared her story with me, fellow angel author Eileen Freeman and workshop leader Caroline Sutherland on a recent edition of The Laura Lee Show in which several striking incidents were discussed.

15. Essay: The Celestial Helper, Unseen to Some, Yet Visible to Others...

"Angels come most commonly, I think, to children, saints and primitive people, to the innocents, who perhaps can perceive more clearly than we."
Sophy Burnham

"See that you don't despise any of these little ones. their angels in heaven, I tell you, are always in the presence of my Father in heaven."
Jesus of Nazareth

O Lord, our Lord, your greatness is seen in all the world... It is sung by children and babies.
Psalm 8

Children, maybe because of their purity and innocence, and lack of preconceived ideas that the realm of the spiritual is "impossible," often see the heavenly while we life-hardened grown-ups go around blindly. No wonder that kids are an important part of this family of stories where the helping angel or guardian spirit is seen by others but not by the person being helped.

Another major category of the unseen helper story involves vulnerable people who avoid being attacked because would-be assailants see a powerful escort with the intended victims which the targeted victims themselves cannot see.

This type of story often crops up in tough neighborhood settings, involving rapists or muggers put off by the sight of an escort; battlefield locales, where a superior force decides not to attack; or remote areas, where defenseless missionaries are threatened by hostile forces.

In her runaway best seller *Where Angels Walk*, Joan Wester Anderson recounts the experience of a young Brooklyn woman walking home by herself through a poor section of town, praying for her guardian angel to protect her when she noticed a threatening man ahead of her. She walked by without incident but later was called to the police station to help in investigating this stranger, who had been arrested for raping a woman at that location a short time after she passed by. The man told police he had not raped the original woman because "two big guys" were at either side of her.

A classic missionary-style story is narrated by the famed evangelist Billy Graham. Graham described how angry natives attacked the mission headquarters of the Rev. John G. Paton in the Pacific Ocean's New Hebrides island chain. Terrified, Paton and his wife prayed through the night and were surprised when the natives left. Months afterward, after relations improved, the local chief told Paton the assault had broken off because the attackers saw hundreds of large, sword-wielding men in shining clothes, circling the mission station. Paton believed these mysterious guards were angels, Graham said.

Battlefield stories, a third sub category, are found as far back as the Old Testament story of the prophet Elisha, protected by a flaming troop of angels against massed Assyrian soldiers -- a celestial phalanx that Elisha's panicky servant had not been able at first to see. "We are doomed, sir!" the servant had cried out, but Elisha calmly replied, "Don't be afraid. We have more on our side than they have on theirs." Then, the servant's eyes were opened so he could share the vision. The Assyrians had been upset with Elisha for psychically divining their military secrets and passing on the intelligence to Israel's king during a war.

The battlefield genre of "seen and unseen" continues in medieval legend. One tale has that barbarian's barbarian Attila the Hun, calling off an attack on Rome after seeing two "shining beings" on either side of Pope Leo as he begged for mercy, something the Romans themselves were unaware of at the time.

Angel Directory

Retail Angel Stores

- A Wing & A Prayer, 2000 Riverchase Galleria, Birmingham AL 35244
- Sincerely Yours, 1555 Camino Del Mar #320, Del Mar CA 92014
- Angels de las Flores, 318 N. Santa Cruz Ave., Los Gatos CA 95030
- Heaven on Earth, 1050 East Walnut Street, Pasadena CA 91106-1419
- Tara's Angels, 31781 Camino Capistrano, San Juan Capistrano CA 92675
- Angels By The Sea, 75 Mt. Hermon Road #C, Scotts Valley CA 95066
- Ark Angels Flowers & Gifts, 116 Main Street, Tiburon CA 94920
- Angels, 135 Center Street, Ste. 8, Manchester CT 06040
- Angels For All Seasons, 3100 So. Sheridan Blvd., Denver CO 80227
- D'Angels Place, 5450 Peachtree Parkway, Ste. 1-A, Norcross GA 30092
- Guardian Angel Shop, Century Mall, 2700 N. Clark Street, Chicago IL (Open from Sept. 15 through January 15)
- Angels Loft, 516 N. Bedford Street, East Bridgewater MA 02333

- Angelica of the Angels, 7 Central Street, Salem MA 01970
- Heavens to Betsy, Bankers Galleria, 8098 Main Street, Ellicott City MD 21043
- Host of Angels, Middletown Mall, Middletown MD 21769
- Angels of Hope, 29 Allegheny Avenue, Towson MD 21204
- Angel Treasures, 401 N. Main, Royal Oak MI 48067
- Presents of Angels, 4404 France Avenue So., Edina MN 55410
- The Angel Shoppe, Biltmore Village, 3 Brook Street, Asheville NC 28803
- Little Angels, 1275 Bloomfield Avenue, Door 1, Fairfield NJ 07004
- Everything Angels, 9 West 31st Street 2-R, New York NY 10001
- Angels & Us and Angel Gallery, 3257 SE Hawthorne Blvd., Portland OR 97214
- Guardian Angels, D209 Trolley Square, 602 East 500 South, Salt Lake City UT 84102
- Among the Angels, 402 Laskin Road, Virginia Beach VA 23451

Mail Order

- The Angel Book Catalog. One of the largest sources of angel books anywhere. For a free copy of the basic catalog, send a stamped (32 cents), self-addressed envelope to Mamre Press, 107-CA South Second Avenue, Murfreesboro TN 37130. To receive the complete catalog, place 55 cents in postage on the SASE.

- Everything Angels, P.O. Box 467, New York NY 10028-0004. A slick and colorful mail-order catalog. The catalog is $2, but it will be deducted from the first order.

- Caroline Sutherland, P.O. Box 70, Hansville WA 98340. Has a doll for children to hold at night and a positive-thinking tape to play along with it, entitled *My Little Angel Tells Me I'm Special.*

- Angels Express. For information on Kathy Krzywicki's catalog of products, write: P.O. Box 8094, Gaithersburg MD 20898.

- Marilynn's Angels, 275 Celeste Drive, Riverside CA 92507. Send $1 for catalog.

Publications

- AngelWatch Journal. An outstanding bimonthly newsletter that reads like a daily newspaper of hard news and features concerning angels. Edited by Eileen Freeman, who holds a masters in theology from Notre Dame and has had a series of dramatic experiences of her own with her guardian angel. Contains a useful resource list, updated with every issue. For information, write: The AngelWatch Foundation, P.O. Box 1397, Mountainside NJ 07092-0397.

- Angel Times. A slick, full-color magazine, professionally done. The inaugural issue featured an interview with the daughter of the late Michael Landon, who played the human-looking angel Jonathan Smith on the old Highway to Heaven TV series; an interview with the producers of a blockbuster

NBC special on angels; and articles by, among others, artist Karyn Martin-Kuri, authors Eileen Freeman and Terry Lynn Taylor, and Sally Allen, who opened the much-publicized Angels For All Seasons shop in Denver. For information, write: Angel Times, 4360 Chamblee-Dunwoody Road, Ste. 400, Atlanta GA 30341.

Organizations

- Angel Collectors Club of America. Founded in 1976, this organization's 1,000-plus members collect angel representations of every type. This includes figurines, ornaments, dolls, angels on postcards, and paper angels. Beyond collecting, the members have a general interest in angelology. They share their angel knowledge in talks before church groups, at retirement homes and in other locations. The ACCA's chatty quarterly newsletter is titled *Halo Everybody!* Members correspond, there are area chapters meeting regularly to talk about places of interest to angel lovers and spots where angel articles can be bought. A national convention is scheduled biennially. For more information, contact Blanche Thompson at 533 E. Fairmont Dr., Tempe AZ 85282.

- Angels of the World. A 200-plus member group devoted to the study and enjoyment of things angelic. Many of these angel enthusiasts are collectors of various angel-oriented items. There are local chapters around the country and a bimonthly newsletter called *Notes and Comments.* For information, write to: Angels of the World, 1334 South Reisner, Indianapolis IN 46221.

- Angel Heights. The yearly Be An Angel Day is the brainchild of Jane Howard's organization. Angel Height's address is P.O. Box 95, Upperco MD 21155.

- Spiritual Frontiers Fellowship International. This interfaith organization of ministers and laity seeks to explore the mounting interest in mystical experience and parapsychology "within and outside the church, wherever these experiences relate to effective prayer, spiritual healing and survival of consciousness." The group has a 12,000-volume library on parapsychology, metaphysics and religion. SFFI conducts several regional summer retreats annually. It also publishes a monthly newsletter and the quarterly Spiritual Frontiers Journal. Address inquiries to SFFI, P.O. Box 7868, Philadelphia PA 19101.

- International Association for Near-Death Studies. This group is concerned with the overall near-death experience, widely discussed in connection with heavenly encounters. IANDS brings together health care professionals, lay people, and of course, those who have had near-death experiences. Within this group, researchers as well as professionals who have encountered the NDE phenomenon can network with one another. This group may be contacted by writing IANDS, P.O. Box 7767, Philadelphia PA 19101.

- 28 Angels. Angel artist K. Martin-Kuri's organization, which has scheduled angel conferences, among other activities. P.O. Box 116, Free Union VA 22940.

Books on Angels & Related Topics

- Adler, Mortimer. The Angels and Us. Macmillan Publishing Co., N.Y. 1982. The famed philosopher provides a well-synthesized summary of centuries of philosophical thinking about angels.

- Anderson, Joan Wester. Where Angels Walk. Barton & Brett, Publishers. Sea Cliff, New York. 1992. A series of compelling stories of particularly dramatic encounters between humans and angels. Warm and inspirational reading.

- Anderson, Joan Wester. Ballantine Books, New York. 1994. An An gel to Watch Over Me. True stories of children's encounters with angels.

- Anderson, Joan Wester. Where Miracles Happen. Brett Books, Brooklyn, N.Y. 1994. Miracle stories, including angel encounters.

- Kirven, Robert H. Angels in Action: What Swedenborg Saw and Heard. Swedenborg Foundation, West Chester, Pa. How the 18th Century mystic and scientist Emanuel Swedenborg perceived the angelic kingdom.

- Begbie, Harold. On the Side of the Angels: A Reply to Arthur Machen. Hodder and Stoughton, London. 1915. A detailed account of the alleged sightings of saints and angels on the western battlefront of Europe during World War I.

- Blackmore, Rev. Simon. The Angel World. John Winterich, Cleveland. 1927.

- Boros, Ladislaus. Angels and Men. Seabury Press, N.Y. 1977.

- Brewer, Rev. Cobham. A Dictionary of Miracles. Gale Research Co., Detroit. 1966. A detailed survey of miracle lore regarding saints, angels and the like, much of it from the Middle Ages.

- Burnham, Sophy. A Book of Angels. Ballantine Books, New York. 1990. A very personal and sensitive book with a beautiful gold foil cover. It soared onto the best seller lists. Many interesting stories, facts and observations.

- Burnham, Sophy. Angel Letters. Ballantine Books, New York. 1991. The popular sequel to A Book of Angels, which inspired many readers to write letters to Ms. Burnham about their own angelic experiences. This is a collection of those letters, with stories told in the writers' own words.

- Cameron, Ann. The Angel Book. Ballantine Books, N.Y. 1977. One of the better general surveys of the angel world.

- Cherubs: Angels of Love. Little, Brown & Co. Boston. A delightful large-format coffee-table book of full-color cherub art, with a 12-page introductory essay by Alexander Nagel.

- Chessman, Harriet. Literary Angels. Ballantine Books, New York. This book helps open up a new genre of angel literature -- an anthology of angel-oriented fiction and poetry, edited by a former Yale University literature instructor. Featured are such writers as Elizabeth Barrett Browning, John Donne, John Updike, Leo Tolstoy, Dante and Mark Twain, among many others.

- Church, F. Forrester. Entertaining Angels. Harper & Row, San Francisco. 1987. A witty and light-hearted look at the world of angels from the eyes of a religious progressive.

- Clement, Clara. Angels in Art. L.C. Page & Co., Boston. 1898. A well-done specialized discussion.

- Connolly, David. In Search of Angels. The Putnam Publishing Group, New York. 1993. Thorough, thoughtful and meticulously researched. Good angel journalism.

- Daniel, Alma; Wyllie Timothy; and Ramer, Andrew. Ask Your Angels. Ballantine Books, N.Y. 1992. The authors describe meditation and visualization techniques and exercises which they recommend for developing a greater awareness of angels.

- Danielou, Jean. The Angels and Their Mission. Christian Classics, Westminster, Maryland. 1957. One of Catholicism's foremost theologians, the French Priest Jean Danielou discusses angels and the sacraments, how angels preside over the growth of the church, the mission of angels, etc. A strength of the book is Danielou's synthesis of the teachings of ancient church fathers with modern theological ideas.

- Davidson, Gustav. A Dictionary of Angels. The Free Press, New York. 1971. A browser's delight for more than two decades. Davidson, the author-editor of a dozen books, spent 15 years researching this 414-page classic. Unsurpassed for angel scholarship (the bibliography covers 25 pages of small type!), this highly recommended volume may be the most detailed and scholarly look at angel folklore and legend in existence.

- Eadie, Betty. Embraced by the Light. Bantam Books, New Yor. One of the more complex near-death experiences that have been reported.

- Ekberg, Susan and Neavill, Michelle. Pink Stars & Angel Wings. Spiritseeker Publishing, Fargo, N.D. 1992. A juvenile book at the second-grade reading level about a young girl's journey to her special star in the sky, where she meets her guardian angel and discovers much about herself and her world.

- Fearheiley, Don. Angels Among Us. Avon Books, New York. 1993. Twelve angel encounter narratives.

- Field. Angels and Ministers of Grace. Hill and Wang, N.Y. 1971.

- Fowler, Alfred. Our Angels Friends in Ministry and Song. (No publisher listed)

- Freeman, Eileen. Touched by Angels. Warner Books, New York. 1993. Eileen Freeman burst onto the national scene in 1992 -- the "year of the angel," when national media reported on a resurgence of interest in angels that had been building momentum for some time. As editor of *AngelWatch Journal,* a periodical reporting hard news and features about angels, Freeman found herself repeatedly behind microphones and in front of TV cameras. Here, she tells how angels personally have touched her life and those of others.

- Freeman, Eileen. Angelic Healing. Warner Books, New York. 1994. As of its publication, this was the only book focusing exclusively on the subject of angels as it relates to the healing of the body and the spirit.

- Freeman, Eileen. The Angels' Little Instruction Book. Warner Books, New York. Illuminating ideas about angels, joined by passages from the Bible.

- Gaebelain, Arno. The Angels of God. Our Hope Publication Office, N.Y. 1924.

- Giovetti, Paola. Angels. An Italian book translated into English, Angels combines Catholic and metaphysical perspectives. Well-written and containing many beautiful full-color plates.

- Gilmore, Don. Angels, Angels Everywhere. Pilgrim, N.Y. 1981.
- Giudici, Maria. The Angels. Alba House, New York. 1993. A Roman Catholic nun's scholarly yet popularly written survey of the subject.
- Godwin, Malcolm. Angels: An Endangered Species. Simon and Shuster, New York. 1990. This large and attractive hardcover book for the coffee table has almost 200 gorgeous illustrations, most of them in color. Fine coverage of angel folklore, spiced with Godwin's wit and whimsy.
- Goldman, Karen. The Angel Book. Simon and Shuster, New York. 1992. An inspirational series of beautiful short thoughts and proverbs on things angelic.
- Graham, Billy. Angels: God's Secret Agents. Pocket Books, N.Y. 1975. The famous evangelist's best-seller presents evangelical Christian opinion about angels. Interlaced with anecdotes.
- Grant, Robert. Are We Listening to the Angels? A.R.E. Press, Virginia Beach, Va. 1994. A book for those with an interest in the ideas of the late famous psychic Edgar Cayce and how those ideas relate to the subject of angels.
- Guiley, Rosemary. Angels of Mercy. Pocket Books, New York. 1994. Particularly interesting reading and also unusually information-rich. Guiley is a veteran researcher and writer on metaphysical subjects.
- Hahn, Emily. Breaths of God. Doubleday & Co., New York. 1971. A sweet and whimsical look at the world of angels, written with a light touch.
- Hall, Manley. The Blessed Angels. The Philosophical Research Society, Los Angeles. 1980.

- Harrison, Margaret. Angels Then and Now. Branch-Smith, Fort Worth. 1975.

- Hodson, Geoffrey. The Brotherhood of Angels and Men. Theosophical Publishing House, Wheaton, Ill. 1982. A favorite of theosophists since its first appearance in 1927, written by a renowned clairvoyant.

- Howard, Jane. Commune with the Angels. A.R.E. Press, Virginia Beach, Va. 1992. The author presents her system for developing an awareness of the angelic presence.

- Huber, Georges. Christian Classics, Westminster, Maryland. 1983.

- Humann, Harvey. The Many Faces of Angels. DeVorss & Co., Publisher, Marina del Rey, Calif. 1986. A thought-provoking basic introduction to the world of angels with many fresh, unconventional ideas on the subject.

- Jameson, Anna. Legends of the Madonna. Longmans, Green and Co., London. 1890.

- Joppie, A.S. The Ministry of Angels. Baker Book House. Grand Rapids, Mich. 1953.

- Latham, Henry. A Service of Angels. Deighton, Bell & Co., Cambridge. 1896.

- Leadbeater, C.W. Invisible Helpers. Theosophical Publishing Concern, Chicago. 1915. Presents the viewpoint that departed human souls, acting like ministering angels, are actively helping rescue, comfort and otherwise minister to us. Contains interesting anecdotes.

- Leavell, Landrum. Angels, Angels, Angels. Broadman Press, Nashville. 1973.

- Lloyd, Marjorie Lewis. It Must Have Been an Angel. Pacific Press Publishing Association, Mountain View, Calif. 1980.

- Lockyer, Herbert. The Mystery and Ministry of Angels. Eerdmans Publishing Co., Grand Rapids, Mich. 1958.

- MacGregor, Geddes. Angels: Ministers of Grace. Paragon House, New York. 1988. The prominent theologian Geddes MacGregor's interesting discussion of angels in art, literature, music, mythology, and the Bible. Among the subjects covered: the possibility that humans may evolve into angels.

- Margolies, Morris. A Gathering of Angels. Margolies, a rabbi and scholar, has produced a very readable and absorbing look at angels from the Jewish perspective.

- McConkie, Oscar, Jr. Angels. Deseret Book Co., Salt Lake City, Utah. 1975. A discussion of angels from the Mormon point of view.

- Malz, Betty. A survey of the subject by a prominent Christian author, whose book My Glimpse of Eternity, sold more than a half million copies.

- Miller, Leslie. All About Angels. Regal Books, Glendale, Calif. 1976.

- Moody, Raymond, Jr. Life After Life. Bantam Books, N.Y. A psychiatrist, Moody collected, offhand for years, scores of personal anecdotes of near-death experiences. In this landmark book, which classified the stages of near-death experiences, Moody notes that near-death survivors often claim to have met brilliant ''beings of light.'' These angel-like entities were prepared to escort them to the Beyond or turn them back to the living.

- Moody, Raymond, Jr. Reflections on Life After Life. Bantam Books, N.Y. 1978. The sequel to Life After Life in which Moody describes how persons brushing with death claim to have glimpsed happy "cities of light."

- Moolenburgh, Hans. A Handbook of Angels. C.W. Daniel Co., Saffron Walden, England. 1984. A wide-ranging and lively discussion by a Dutch surgeon who made headlines in Holland in connection with angels. Moolenburgh conducted an informal survey of 400 of his patients to see how frequently ordinary people see angels. Eight per cent claimed to have had the experience.

- Moolenburgh, Hans. Meetings With Angels. C.W. Daniel Co., Saffron Walden, England. 1992. One hundred and one angel encounter stories, based on letters written to the author in response to A Handbook of Angels.

- Morse, Melvin and Paul Perry. Closer to the Light. Ballantine Books, New York. 1990. A pediatrician's touching investigation of the near-death experiences of children he interviewed. This popular book is based on a study which was published in the pediatric journal of the American Medical Association.

- Mould, Daphne. Angels of God. Devin-Adair Co., N.Y. 1963.

- Newhouse, Flower. Natives of Eternity. J.F. Rowny Press, Santa Barbara, Calif. 1937. A theosophical clairvoyant describes her visions of the angel world.

- Nyberg, Joan. Wingtip Press, St. Paul. 1994. A Rustling of Wings: An Angelic Guide to the Twin Cities. An outstanding guidebook for angel enthusiasts wanting to meet the "angels" of the St. Paul-Minneapolis urban area: Angel art in museums, churches; regional artists; local angel encounter stories; and a lot more.

- O'Sullivan, Paul. All About the Angels. A well-written pocket-sized book treating the subject in the Roman Catholic tradition. Tan Books, Rockford, Ill. 1990.

- Palmer, Tobias. An Angel in my House. Ave Maria Press, Notre Dame, Ind. 1975.

- Parente, Alessio. Send Me Your Guardian Angel. Editions Carlo Tozza Napoli. 1984. Recounts the life of the famous Catholic priest Padre Pio, who told those requesting his help to send him their guardian angel if they could not come themselves.

- Parente, Pascal. Beyond Space. Tan Books, Rockford, Ill. 1973. A popularly written Roman Catholic exposition of angels by a leading theologian and priest.

- Parisen, Maria (Compiler). Angels and Mortals. Theosophical Publishing House. Wheaton, Ill. 1990. A collection of mostly metaphysically oriented articles by prominent authors. Topics include the mystic Emanuel Swedenborg's reports of angel encounters, the native American holy man Black Elk's visionary ascent to heaven, Mohammed's vision of Gabriel, etc.

- Paula, Mary. Presenting the Angels. Benziger Brothers. 1935.

- Regamy, Raymond. What is an Angel? Hawthorn Books, N.Y. 1960.

- Richards, H.M.S., Jr. Angels -- Secret Agents of God and Satan. Review and Herald Publishing Association, Nashville. 1980.

- Ritchie, George. Return From Tomorrow. Baker Book House, Grand Rapids, Mich. 1978. A page-turner. Ritchie is the ''grandfather'' of the near-death experience -- an inspiration to Raymond Moody to begin his own NDE work. Ritchie's near-death experience and visit to heavenly and hellish realms is among the most detailed and interesting on record.

- Ring, Kenneth. Life at Death. Coward, McCann and Geoghegan, N.Y. After Raymond Moody's pioneering classification of the stages of the near-death experience (NDE), Ring and others conducted scientific investigations of the NDE phenomenon.

- Ronner, John. Do You Have a Guardian Angel? Mamre Press, Murfreesboro, Tenn. 1985. Fourteen months of research condensed into a journalistic-style question-and-answer format.

- Ronner, John. Know Your Angels: The Angel Almanac. Mamre Press, Murfreesboro, Tenn. 1993. An almanac of alphabetically arranged articles on myriad aspects of the subject of angels. Plus, dozens of "biographies" of individual angel personalities -- such as Michael, Gabriel and Raphael -- drawn from angel folklore, legend and mythology.

- Sabom, Michael. Recollections of Death: A Medical Investigation. Harper & Row, N.Y. 1982. Sabom conducted one of several scientifically oriented studies of the near-death experience.

- St. Michael and the Angels. Tan Books and Publishers, Rockford, Ill. 1983.

- Smith, Robert. In the Presence of Angels. A.R.E. Press, Virginia Beach, Va. Angelic experiences gathered in a research project among the followers of the readings and work of the late famous psychic Edgar Cayce.

- Steiger, Brad and Steiger, Sherry. Angels Over Their Shoulders. Popular authors Brad and Sherry Steiger offer their own collection of children encounter stories.

- Taylor, Terry Lynn. Messengers of Light. H.J. Kramer, Tiburon, Calif. 1990. Taylor's positive and upbeat best-seller combines angels and self-help.

- Guardians of Hope. H.J. Kramer, Tiburon, Calif. Taylor's sequel to Messengers of Light and its concepts.

- Taylor, Terry Lynn. Answers From the Angels. H.J. Kramer, Tiburon, Calif. 1993. Taylor received thousands of letters from readers of Messengers of Light, much of the mail describing correspondents' experiences with angels. This is a selection from the mailbag, with stories told in the writer's own words.

- Taylor, Terry Lynn. Creating With the Angels. H.J. Kramer, Tiburon, Calif. 1993. How angel consciousness can be used to awaken creativity.

- Tyler, Kelsey. There's an Angel on Your Shoulder. The Berkley Publishing Group, N.Y. 1994. A collection of true life angel encounter stories from a Christian perspective.

- Ward, Theodora. Men and Angels. Viking Press, N.Y. 1969. A well-written general survey of the angel world, with several glossy sections of illustrations by classic artists.

- Westermann, Claus. God's Angels Need No Wings. Fortress Press. 1979.

- Webber, Marilynn and William. A Rustle of Angels. Messenger angels, warrior angels, angels at the time of death. Encounter stories sorted by category -- by well-known Christian writer Marilyn Webber and her husband, who has a doctorate in theology.

- Wilson, Peter. Angels. Pantheon Books, N.Y. 1980. A nicely illustrated coffee table book. Wilson does a particularly good job of crossing cultures as he

examines angelology. He is especially informative
about Muslim lore concerning angels.

Video

- Life After Life. Cascom International, Nashville. 1992.
  A captivating 57-minute video based on the
  best-selling book by Raymond Moody chronicling the
  stages of the near-death experience.

CD-ROM

- Angels: The Mysterious Messengers. An interactive
  odyssey. Experiencers discussing their own moving
  encounters; angel art; reference material; networking
  information about newsletters and groups. Live
  Interactive, 100 Fusion Way, Country Club Hills IL
  60478.

Cassette

- Do You Have a Guardian Angel? Mamre Press,
  Murfreesboro, Tenn. 1993. Cassette version of the
  book (described above).
- Know Your Angels. Mamre Press, Murfreesboro,
  Tenn. 1993. Cassette version of the book (described
  above).
- Angelology: A Heavenly Experience. A 59-minute talk
  about angels from a metaphysical perspective by Unity
  Church pastor Carolyn Crane.

Index

Do You Have a Guardian Angel?

Here is a 188-page book with hundreds of amazing facts: How angels guide, rescue and protect us. Where and when we see angels. How angels escort us when we die. How angels are contacted. Strong evidence that angels exist. Do angels keep our universe working? What are fallen angels? Who's who in heaven and hell?

These are just a few of the hundreds of fascinating topics in best-selling author John Ronner's thoroughly researched boo, *Do You Have a Guardian Angel?* The book is jam-packed with eye-opening facts, stories, quotes and figures.

Read about:

The ghostly armies of World War I; Emanuel Swedenborg, a world famous scientist who went into trances for days at a time to visit the spirit world and talk with angels; an endangered Mt. Everest climber who suddenly became aware of a strong, friendly but invisible companion; an Ohio boarding house where an extra place was regularly set at the huge dining table -- for an angel.

Besides true stories, *Do You Have a Guardian Angel?* is a condensed encyclopedia of amusing and bizarre angel legends, folklore and myths. The book has more than 30 stunning full-page illustrations by classic artists and a detailed index and bibliography for reference value.

Available at your bookstore or send $10.95 plus $1.80 shipping to: Mamre Press, P.O. Box 3137, Murfreesboro TN 37133-3137.

Know Your Angels: Meet 100 Prominent Angels From Legend & Folklore

Who's who in heaven and hell? Here is a book to answer that question: An alphabetical listing of biographies of 100 prominent angels drawn from scripture, legend, folklore and mythology. Michael, Gabriel, Raphael, Uriel, Metatron, Mithra, Lucifer, Sophia, the Dark Angel who wrestled with the Bible patriarch Jacob -- they're all here. But the book has much more than angel profiles. there are also many entries for angel-related topics like the legendary war in heaven, the different opinions about how angels

fell, the seven heavens, Moses' visit to heaven, the angel who guided Socrates, Jewish, Christian, Muslim and Zoroastrian angels, etc.

An invaluable reference work of hard-to-find information all "under one roof" for the angel enthusiast, minister or teacher, or those who want specific information on particular angels:

Who is the patron angel of travelers? Of writers? Of police officers? And why?

Which angels oversee which countries?

Which angel's birthday was used as the date to celebrate Christmas and how did it happen?

Which angel guides newly dead souls in the afterlife?

Who is the angel of healing?

Available at your bookstore or send $10.95 plus $1.80 shipping to: Mamre Press, P.O. Box 3137, Murfreesboro TN 37133-3137.

Angel Books Now Also on Cassette Tape

Now John Ronner's popular angel books are available on cassette. Each cassette has a 55-minute reading by the author of key passages:

- Do You Have a Guardian Angel? (cassette) $9.95

- Know Your Angels (cassette) $9.95

- The Angels of Cokeville $9.95

Available at your bookstore or send $9.95 each plus $1.80 shipping for the first tape and 60 cents for each additional tape to Mamre Press, P.O. Box 3137, Murfreesboro TN 37133-3137.

About the Author

John Ronner, a 43-year-old writer, is the husband of a Presbyterian minister and the father of two primary school daughters. A former newspaper reporter, John won repeated awards for his writing from organizations ranging from The Associated Press to United Press International. John's work has been praised by reviewers, including Publishers Weekly, and he has appeared on many national, regional and local shows in recent years, including the NBC special, Angels II. A dynamic speaker, John has addressed the subject of heavenly intervention before diverse audiences. To inquire about having John as a speaker, write for details to: Mamre Press, Attn.: Dian Rhodes, P.O. Box 3137, Murfreesboro TN 37130.